GW00702735

Doing it with
Doris

Doing it with Doris

Kate Turkington

PENGUIN BOOKS

PENGUIN BOOKS

Published by the Penguin Group
80 Strand, London WC2R 0RL, England
Penguin Putnam Inc, 375 Hudson Street, New York, New York
10014, USA
Penguin Books Australia Ltd, 250 Camberwell Road, Camberwell,
Victoria 3124, Australia
Penguin Books Canada Ltd, 10 Alcorn Avenue, Toronto, Ontario,
Canada M4V 3B2
Penguin Group (NZ), Cnr Airborne and Rosedale Roads, Albany,
Auckland 1310, New Zealand
Penguin Books India (P) Ltd, 11 Community Centre, Panchsheel Park,
New Delhi – 110 017, India
Penguin Books (South Africa) (Pty) Ltd, 24 Sturdee Avenue, Rosebank,
Johannesburg 2196, South Africa

Penguin Books (South Africa) (Pty) Ltd, Registered Offices:
24 Sturdee Avenue, Rosebank, Johannesburg 2196, South Africa

First published by Penguin Books (South Africa) (Pty) Ltd 2004

Copyright © Kate Turkington 2004

All rights reserved
The moral right of the author has been asserted

ISBN 0 143 02444 2

Typeset by CJH Design in 11/14 pt Aldine
Cover design: African Icons
Printed and bound by Interpak Books, Pietermaritzburg

Except in the United States of America, this book is sold subject to the
condition that it shall not, by way of trade or otherwise, be lent,
resold, hired out or otherwise circulated without the publisher's prior
consent in any form of binding or cover other than that in which it is
published and without a similar condition including this condition
being imposed on the subsequent purchaser.

*To three great friends
who have made the journey with me:*

*Vicki Ironmonger
Marié Craig
Sylvia Gill*

Acknowledgements

My thanks go to the Virtuoso of Virgos at Penguin South Africa, who made the road smoother . . . Alison Lowry, Pam Thornley and Claire Heckrath.

And to my always loving and supportive family – past, present and future.

I'm also grateful to my stained, white ant-chewed copy of *Mary Slessor, The White Queen* by W P Livingstone (Hodder & Stoughton, 1931).

Contents

1

Doing it with Doris

Doris wore black satin knickers until the day she died. At eighty-nine going on forty.

'Because,' she would say, her brown eyes sparkling with fun and mischief, 'you never know . . .'

Doris always hated the name Doris. She thought it was common. In later life, when she met somebody for the first time, she introduced herself as 'Kathy', a name that she thought sounded much 'posher' and that patently didn't suit her.

Doris was born at the beginning of the twentieth century when names like Doris, Ellen, Marjorie, Dorothy and Mona were all the rage. Flower names were popular too – Rose and Violet, Primrose and Poppy. It was a time of hackney carriages and horse buses, hobble skirts and big hats overloaded with ostrich and egret feathers, doctors in frock coats and tea clippers bringing England staples and luxury goods from far-flung places. Gas-inflated airships flew overhead whilst gas sizzled and spat in the streetlights below. Women knew their place – in the kitchen, bedroom, front parlour or filling in a dance card, depending on their social status. God was in Heaven and everything was right with the British world and its incredible Empire. It was OK to enslave other people – in mines, factories and sweatshops – both at home and abroad. Britannia Ruled the Waves. No question of it. And the hierarchy of British society was as firmly entrenched as was the unquestionable belief that British was Best.

Doris was the fifth child of a former Swedish sea captain, Johan Ferdinand Ahlquist and his Yorkshire-born wife Edith, who came from a long line of Yorkshire witches. How successful her female forebears were as witches is debatable because the family name was Ashburn.

When Johan's windjammer was caught in a terrible snowstorm in the Gulf of St Lawrence, he fell 140 feet from aloft and sustained severe injuries, including a compound fracture of the leg and three broken ribs. There was no doctor on board and so Johan remained without any medical attention for two months while the ship sailed on its leisurely way to Buenos Aires. Once there, arrangements were made to send him to Greenwich Hospital in London.

Whilst recovering from these injuries at Greenwich (he walked with a slight limp for the rest of his life), he made use of the period of inactivity to learn to speak and write perfect English. He also met and wooed Edith who was one of his nurses. She fell in love with the tall, blond, blue-eyed Viking and, after a whirlwind romance, they were married in the local registry office.

Edith's family, the Ashburns, took all these happenings in their stride, and Great-Aunt Sarah, who had been a Gaiety Girl on the Music Hall, which gave her much local notoriety, read the tea leaves, spun her crystal ball, got out the Tarot cards and announced that a great and grand line would come from this match.

Great-Aunt Sarah's predictions were often proved right in spite of a blinkered judgement of men. She had embarked on a disastrous affair with an English Earl, a stereotypical 'Stage Door Johnny' who waited at the stage door of the theatre every night, moustachioed and silken-cravated, with a bunch of flowers in his pigskin-gloved hand, to pick up and woo the prettiest and most popular chorus girl. Great-Aunt Sarah, with the longest, loveliest legs, dark ringlets, dancing eyes and cheeky wit, had no peer.

However, her upbringing in a stone cottage on the Yorkshire Moors had not prepared her for the duplicities of the English aristocracy set on seduction. She fell in love, believed she would become a Countess, fell pregnant and was abandoned. She adored her only son Charlie, the fruit of the Earl's lustful loins, who would have been umpteenth in line to the British Throne had he been legitimised, as she told anybody who would listen or was not scandalised by her saucy, forward behaviour. Instead, Charlie took the King's Shilling and became a sergeant major of note in the Coldstream Guards.

Armed only with Great-Aunt Sarah's optimistic predictions, young love, cleverness and driving ambition, and without a penny to their name, Johan and Edith made it to London where they finally ended up in a tall, three-storeyed house on London's Isle of Dogs, now the trendy Canary Wharf district. Here they raised five children. Frank, the oldest, enlisted for World War I at the age of fifteen, returning home shell-shocked and trauma-tised after spending three days on the battlefield at Ypres lying wounded among thousands of dead men. As children, we were never allowed to raise our voices when Uncle Frank came to visit.

'It's his nerves,' my mother would whisper enigmatically.

Phyllis, the oldest girl, was an early and ardent feminist, who took up a nursing career. She visited Germany in the late Thirties with a group of women from her circle, and used to tell my sister Rita and me how appalled and shocked she was by the Nazi storm troopers and their treatment of the Jews. She had seen an old man with a beard knocked down and spat upon in a Berlin street. For the rest of her life she hated Germans. Next in line were the twins, John and Edith, impossibly good-looking and blond and blue-eyed like their Swedish father. John, an active socialist, emigrated to Australia in the Thirties and became a candidate for the Australian Labour Party, and Edith, following in the footsteps of Great-Aunt Sarah, took to the boards, repeated family history by having an illicit affair with yet another noble scion of the British aristocracy, and died giving birth to illegitimate twins. Doris, my mother, known to her adoring family as 'The Golden Pig', was the youngest and most thoroughly spoilt. Assorted animals completed the household, including a shrieking sulphur-crested cockatoo and an untrainable monkey from the Spanish island of Fernando Póo off the West Coast of Africa, that was so devoted to Edith it clung round her neck in a semi-permanent position.

When Doris felt she wasn't getting enough attention from her adored mother, she would lisp prettily, fat sausage ringlets trembling, 'My Mama loves that monkey more than me!'

Tears would be squeezed out of her dark brown eyes until Edith swooped her up in her arms, trying at the same time to disentangle the clinging monkey and reassure her beloved Golden Pig. Family history does not record the outcomes of these sessions of emotional blackmail, or who won – my mother or the monkey. My money is on Doris.

My grandfather started work as a humble docker in the East India Dock, and rose to become the Dock's Manager, no mean feat in the xenophobic England of the day.

Circumstances, a world at war, not once, but twice in fairly quick succession, made the travel of my mother's dreams impossible. But, having grown up with tales of the sea and far-flung places, with dark-complexioned strangers and burly Scandinavian visitors seemingly omnipresent in the house, exotic fruits and gooey chewy things brought as presents to the curious children, and tea clippers and ocean-going ships slipping in and out of the docks, Doris was always determined to travel herself. There was a world waiting to be discovered where the sun always shone, brightly coloured birds darted through a jungle landscape, and dreams came true.

And travel she did – to the Old World and the New – to the Highlands of Papua and New Guinea, to the hot springs of Rotorua in New Zealand, to the dusty dorps of Africa, to the green hills of Ireland and the stony deserts of Saudi Arabia and the Red Heart of Australia.

World War II changed many people's lives. In particular, it changed the life of Doris and Dick, my father. Dick, from Tyneside, had been down the mines since the age of fourteen, and had taken part in the infamous Jarrow Hunger March when thousands of miners and factory workers had marched down to London from the north of England to protest their conditions of work and pay. He remembered fainting from hunger and being supported by two older fellow miners. Settling in London, he met and married Doris, before developing consumption from working in an unhealthy and dangerous paint factory in London's East End.

My older sister Rita and I, dressed in home-made pink coats

modelled on those of the Little Princesses, Elizabeth and Margaret, were taken to visit him at a sanatorium somewhere in the country. I remember picking a bunch of wild goldenrod flowers and giving it to him, as he greeted us in the bare ward in his striped pyjamas. We wore berets cocked at a jaunty angle and a photograph of the time shows us proudly saluting 'For King and Country'. Soon afterwards, my father was declared cured and sent home.

But War with a capital W was imminent. Knots of people gathered in the streets. Adults worried and whispered. And then it happened. My mother, always one to make capital out of an occasion, solemnly sat us all down in the front parlour. As this lace-curtained little cocoon was reserved for special occasions only, we knew something was up. My father turned the radio on. It was 11.15 am on Sunday, 3 September 1939, one day after Doris' thirty-fifth birthday. I remember listening to Prime Minister Joseph Chamberlain on that old cat's whisker radio. I was four years old, my sister six. I instinctively knew that something very important was happening. I crossed my feet in their patent leather shoes and assumed a serious expression. Like Doris, I've always been a good judge of the moment. The airwaves crackled and popped. Static squeaked round the room but finally the reedy, scratchy voice of Joseph Chamberlain filled the little room.

> *This country is at war with Germany . . . the government have made plans under which it will be possible to carry on with the work of the nation in the days of stress and strain that may be ahead. But these plans need your help.*
>
> *You may be taking your part in the fighting services or as a volunteer in one of the branches of civil defence . . . You may be*

engaged in work essential to the prosecution of war – in factories, in transport, in public utility concerns, or in the supply of other necessities of life . . .

My mother and father exchanged pregnant glances and my mother caught her breath. The static fizzled in and out.

Now may God bless you all. May he defend the right. It is the evil things that we shall be fighting against – brute force, bad faith, injustice, oppression and persecution – and against them I am certain that the right will prevail.

Doris turned to my father and said, 'We've got to get out of London. And quick!'

In the mean time, she went out and bought Rita and me two tin hats, opportunistically available at the local toyshop. School became very exciting with air raid practices on a daily basis. Down we went, with our foul-smelling rubber gas masks, into the newly dug school air-raid shelter. We sat on long wooden benches and practised putting our gas masks on, and how to lie flat on the floor if a bomb were to go off, and learned jolly patriotic songs.

The Headmaster had a tin of anti-gas ointment for emergency use against mustard gas splashes on the skin. Very, very hi-tech for its day. It made us feel very important. We handed the tin around reverently. The label read <u>OINTMENT ANTI-GAS NO. 2</u>. Apply freely to affected portion of skin <u>AS SOON AS POSSIBLE</u>. Rub in until ointment is absorbed. <u>AVOID CONTACT WITH EYES</u>. We gaped and gawped at this miraculous potion. We were truly in safe hands. The practice session always ended with a spirited rendering of God Save

The King. This was much better than arithmetic.

Then, along with almost one and a half million other London children, Rita and I were evacuated – separated from our homes and families to protect us from the danger of enemy bombing. It was no idle threat. The London Blitz is now legendary, and to give you an idea of just how many people were affected, just over a year later, in November 1940 alone, over four and a half thousand people died in Britain from air bombardment.

Our parents were terrified for our safety. Every day in those first few weeks of war we went to school with our cases packed and brown parcel labels with our printed names pinned on to us, not knowing when or where we would go. Then the day came. For some children evacuation was an adventure, with the opportunity to sample country life for the first time; others, billeted on unsympathetic foster parents, suffered the miseries of loneliness and homesickness. I remember the great glass-domed London railway station where thousands of children were assembled. I remember straw on the floor of the train.

We were sent to the flat, bleak fenlands of East Anglia. For the six months that we lived with strangers away from our loving and caring parents, six-year-old Rita claimed that we were ill-treated. All that I remember is being cold and hungry. Otherwise I can recall nothing of that time my sister and I spent in those desolate, wet, windy marshlands. A case of what a psychiatrist would call Classic Block Out. As we get older, they say our long-term memory returns. I often wonder if I will ever remember what really happened. I'd like to know the truth. Did that unspeakable, unremembered time forge who I am today? Does some of my strength come from those unknown days when, as a four-year-old, not understanding why my parents had deserted me, I had to bite my lip and 'get on with it'?

But I'm sure, even in those dark days, I must have remembered my mother's rallying call: 'If you want something to happen, then make it happen. It's up to you!'

I wanted to go home so desperately that I knew I could make it happen by setting my mind on it.

'If you want to go to the moon,' Doris would tell my sister and me, 'then go there. It's up to you!'

This at a time when England was locked in deadly combat with one of the most vicious tyrants the world has known – Adolf Hitler – and his armies were massing on the shores of Europe ready to invade our sceptr'd isle.

It's nearly winter and we're standing in our small garden in Hertfordshire where the full moon is glittering down on our potatoes, runner beans and rabbit-nibbled cabbages. My mother has taken the nation's plea 'Dig For Victory!' to heart. Out have come the dahlias, dandelions and delphiniums (the primroses, violets and daffodils escape because they are buried under a sprinkling of snow) and in have gone the vegetables that will help us defeat the Hun. We are in full agricultural mode. Fluffy day-old chicks have been brought home from the market in cardboard boxes and placed on the hearth in the flickering firelight to keep warm. My mother's eyes shine as she imagines the baskets full of freshly laid eggs, and then, when the hens are past their productive stage, well, into the pot with them! (The ones who survive never get eaten, of course. They become family pets and poop all over the kitchen floor.)

'Let's get a goat,' she gaily cries, now totally in Farmer Giles mode.

We get a goat called Salome. Salome has been a cosseted pet

goat and tries to sit on all our laps. This is difficult as she is as big as a small pony. None of us, especially my mother, knows that for a goat to give milk, it needs to have kids first. Salome goes back to her pining, previous owner, but my mother's unshakeable faith never falters.

'Make up your minds to do something, and then do it!' Again and again she reiterates through the long, happy days of my post-evacuation childhood. 'It's up to you!'

War brought major freedom to Britain's working class women. They joined the Armed Forces, became ambulance drivers, air-raid wardens, farm workers, mechanics, operated mobile canteens and worked in factories making armaments. Social hierarchies crumbled as people of all shapes, sizes and classes put their back into the War Effort.

After six months Rita and I had been 'rescued' from evacuation and reunited with our parents in a little three-bedroomed, semi-detached house in the countryside outside St Albans in Hertfordshire. As Doris had wisely realised, they had to get out of London. And quick!

Doris went to work on an aircraft assembly line at De Havilland's Aircraft Factory at Hatfield where my father was employed as a welder. In no time, she became a skilled aircraft fitter. By the time Winston Churchill was exhorting the population to 'maintain a spirit of alert and confident energy', something my mother did without trying, Doris and Dick had started a new life. They enjoyed the war years. Because of the TB, my father had been pronounced physically unfit for the armed services and, unlike so many of my friends' fathers, was safely in the bosom of his family.

Apart from the occasional bomb dropping in the neighbourhood, and the ubiquitous chilling whoop of the nightly air-raid warnings, we felt reasonably safe and secure. We were a united family again. There was more money to spend than ever before, and exciting things were always happening. To mark the American entry into the war, underwear embroidered with the American flag went on sale. My mother had a gorgeous pair of silk cami-knickers sporting the Stars and Stripes. Heaven knows where she had got the coupons to buy them. Clothes rationing was strict – if you used your coupons to buy a pair of stockings say every two and a half months, you could buy a dress every nine months, some undies every four months and a nightdress every four years.

Notwithstanding, my mother's cami-knickers were brought out of the pre-war tissue paper that protected them and proudly displayed on the day my cousin Joyce, devastatingly attractive in her WAAF (Women's Auxiliary Air Force) uniform brought some GIs home. Not only did these young American servicemen give us chewing gum and an orange (an orange! I had never seen one before!) but also they vaulted over the front gate and – wait for it – one of them was black! This was the first time in my life that I had seen a real black person and I was thrilled and enchanted. I still remember his name. It was Washington – 'Call me Wash!' – and he came from South Carolina. I rushed off to find South Carolina in my much-thumbed school atlas that, in those days, still had lots of large pink patches of the British Empire all over it.

The war dragged on and finally came to an end. We had a street party to celebrate Italy's Unconditional Surrender ('What's an unconditional surrender?' I kept asking, but nobody explained). On VE Day – Victory in Europe – our parents, always ones to be in the thick of it, took Rita and me up to

London to join in and experience the celebrations.

It was quite a mission. A walk, followed by a bus ride, followed by a steam train ride, followed by a ride in a tube train on London's Underground. But what an occasion! In Whitehall, along with thousands of other celebrating people, we cheered Churchill, the architect of victory. Later, as we sang and danced in Trafalgar Square, where strangers threw their arms round one another, and everybody seemed to be kissing, I thought that the world was packed with happy people, that the bright lights would shine for ever and never go out, and that we, with the rest of the world, would live happily and peacefully ever after.

The Germans and Japanese safely beaten, now there was nothing to stop Doris doing what she had always dreamed of doing – travelling. Armed with six tins of Nescafé, ten pairs of nylon stockings bought on the black market, five pounds that she had saved from the housekeeping money, and unquestioning faith in her own abilities and her Viking blood, my mother set sail for Europe. She had never before left the shores of England.

'I'll only be gone for two weeks,' she announced to her startled husband and daughters. 'I've always wanted to go to Paris. You girls are old enough to look after yourselves and get yourselves off to school. There's a tin of spam in the pantry and don't forget to feed the dog.'

And, whoosh! She was gone.

*

After a Channel crossing from hell, where she throws up non-stop from the White Cliffs of Dover to the coves of Calais, Doris gets off the train at the Gare du Nord in Paris, fortified by some cognac that a dapper elderly French gentleman has insisted on her taking.

'Purely medicinal,' he assures her in a charming French accent, putting a fatherly arm round her. Doris recognises a come-on when she sees one, drinks down the cognac in 'one foul swoop' (one of her many malapropisms), pretends to throw up in one of her Granny's lace handkerchiefs (still today something of a family heirloom), and rushes for the WC. When she comes back, Monsieur X and his flask of brandy are gone.

Now what? Her knowledge of Paris is sketchy, derived only from Pathé Pictorial newsreels of the Allies liberating Paris (she doesn't like the look of the Russians, however) and a lifelong obsession with Toulouse-Lautrec and his muse, La Goulue. So where else should she go but to Montmartre? She takes a taxi to the Moulin Rouge, and on payment of one of her precious tins of Nescafé (worth a small fortune in post-war Paris), Jean the taxi driver promises to ferry her around Paris every morning for a week. On that first day, as they drive round the narrow streets, a little sign catches her eye – *Pension Dickens*. My mother, an ardent fan of Charles Dickens, has read all of his novels and most of his magazine stories and knows she has come to the right place.

The owners, Monsieur and Madame Fleury, take Doris into their modest little establishment and into their hearts. Through sign language, broken English and a smattering of schoolgirl French, they discuss their families, the war, the world and, most of all, the works of Dickens. *A Tale of Two Cities* is one of their favourites. Madame Fleury takes Doris to the Bastille, and shows her where Sydney Carton would have stepped out on to the scaffold and placed his head in the mouth of La Guillotine as Madame Defarge knitted furiously below, waiting for the head

13

to fall into the basket. It's not hard to imagine Doris and Madame Fleury as they look at one another and simultaneously quote, 'It is a far, far better thing that I do, than I have ever done . . .' as they imagine the dissolute (but sexy) Carton nobly giving up his life to save Charles Darnay and the hapless Lucie. Both of which characters, with exquisite literary judgement, Doris and Mde. Fleury pronounce 'boring'.

After the first week, Doris, Jean, and M. and Mde. Fleury are inseparable. The *pension* owners take turns on a daily basis to see the sights of Paris with my mother, and even though this is a Paris in her post-war tatters, the wonders are still there. The Place de la Concorde, the Champs-Elysées, Notre Dame, the Louvre ('But it's so *small*,' says Doris, gazing unbelievably at the Mona Lisa), the Eiffel Tower, the Left Bank, where they sip Pernod and Doris fancies herself as some latter day artist's companion. She visits the grave of Vaslav Nijinsky in the small Montmartre cemetery (she once saw him dance in London) and walks along the Seine. She sells the coffee (although two tins go to the Fleurys) and buys herself a smart little dress and a chic hat with a veil.

After two weeks it's time to go home, but the Fleurys are about to take their annual vacation in the South. So Doris volunteers to stay on in Montmartre and mind the shop. With no experience of running a *pension*, with hardly a word of French, with just enough money to get by on (but still a few pairs of sought-after nylons), Doris becomes a Parisian hotelier.

She wanted to go to Paris. She made it happen. She did it.

I forget how word came back to us in the English countryside that she was staying on in Paris for another two weeks. But at last she walks down Firwood Avenue, to our Number Sixty-Nine, and the lace curtains of the neighbours twitch as they ooh and aah at Doris in her saucy Parisian clothes. All Rita and I know is that our wonderful mother (not at all like the other mothers we know) is home again. She brings me a little white fox fur collar (still politically correct in those days), and for Rita, a slim black pencil skirt. Dick gets three bottles of the best French wine – a present from the Fleurys – and for the first time in his life he tastes Beaujolais and French champagne.

I was not yet in my teens, but Doris had provided a living lesson to her daughters – the first of many – that if you want something badly enough, it's up to you to make it happen.

*

When my father died suddenly and shockingly at forty-seven, Doris now took off for real. She decided to emigrate to Australia where her brother John, the erstwhile Labour Party candidate, had gone to live all those long years ago.

'What will you do? How will you live?' asked Rita.

We had both won open university scholarships and Rita was now in her second year of university, I in my first. Auntie Phyllis, Doris' sister (who still hated Germans), had offered us a home during our vacations. Phyllis was now the matron of a London mental hospital.

'Look, girls,' responded Doris, 'I'm not yet middle-aged, I'm healthy and quite capable of supporting myself. I feel I must do what I've always wanted to do, to travel to the far distant places I've always dreamed about.'

A few weeks later, as the ship taking her to Australia moved slowly from the docks, a great thrill ran through my mother. This was the real start of her adventures and the realisation of her dreams.

What lay before her she didn't know. But she was to become the personal maid of the wife of the then Governor General of Australia, the fabled war hero, General Sir William Slim. She was to tour all of Australia, from the sheep farms of the remote Outback and the stately cities of Melbourne and Canberra, to the Snowy Mountains, Kakadu, the Northern Territory, and the great inland deserts. She was later to live and work in New Guinea, where the local tribesmen followed the Cargo Cult and her cook sported a large bone through his nose and a bird-of-paradise headdress; New Zealand, where she was the cook on a huge sheep station (she was a terrible cook so I'm not sure how she held that particular job down); a barmaid in the Bronx; and finally after many, many years of travelling, of adventures and misadventures, she came to roost in a little flat outside Brighton in England.

However, there was one more adventure waiting for her. At the age of seventy-four she went off to Saudi Arabia to be nanny to the children of an oil sheikh. She didn't like children and she'd never been a nanny, but those considerations would never stop Doris.

'Why are you going?' Rita and I asked her.

'Because I've never been there and I've always fancied the idea of deserts and I've never met a sheikh.'

Off she went and spent a year there. But that's another story altogether.

At the age of eighty-nine Doris still had boyfriends, wore black satin underwear, and played the piano in an Old Folks' Home, because she said she 'felt sorry for the old people'.

My husband Alan and I were on our way from South Africa to the States to see one of our daughters graduate with a Master's degree in journalism. We left Heathrow Airport and drove to

Brighton. Doris was sitting on her bed in her spick-and-span little flat complaining of a pain in her heart. She had never been ill in her life. Twenty-four hours later she died in my arms with a smile of such serenity and love on her face that I realised, perhaps for the first time, that death can be a joyous experience.

Six months before, my sister Rita had flown from Australia to spend Christmas with Doris. Mother and daughter had spent a blissfully happy day in London, going to a theatre matinée and then buying a hamper of Christmas goodies from Harrods. At home, they enjoyed a sumptuous Christmas Eve supper, but decided to save one special goodie – a tin of duck pâté – for Christmas Day. But it never got eaten – I'll tell you why later. So when Doris heard that Alan and I were to visit her on our way to America, she suggested we could eat the duck pâté from the hamper – she'd been saving it for a special occasion.

'It will be such a treat!' she told me on the phone to Johannesburg. 'I lo-ove duck pâté!'

As she lay dying in my arms in the Royal Sussex Hospital in Brighton, she looked up at me and her brown eyes twinkled.

'It's a pity about the duck pâté!'

So we ate it at her funeral.

She would have liked that.

2

The Pyres of Pashupathinath

And now I want you to come with me on a journey. Together we will meet some amazing and memorable fellow travellers, hear their stories and share their experiences. I want you to leave your baggage at home, because in the course of this journey with me you're going to need space – in your arms, in your mind and in your heart.

Together we are going to travel not only the vast reaches of the physical world, but also the unknown valleys and hills of another world, one that lies behind and beyond our eyes.

Maybe you've been waiting to make such a journey all your life. Maybe you're already on the way. Maybe you haven't even started. Maybe you are too busy, or too anxious. Maybe you believe that it's the wrong time to go. But let's make this particular journey together and see what happens. When it is over, we will go home again.

All the people on this journey are real, and all the stories are true.

It's time . . . Let's go.

Doris would have been proud of me. Like her, I've made things happen, taken opportunities and have lived life to the full.

I've been a writer, a journalist, a magazine editor and a broadcaster for a long time. I've written several academic books and one best-selling mainstream one, *There's More To Life Than Surface* (published by Penguin in 1998). Maybe you've read that one. I've travelled the world writing feature stories about far-flung places and filling my notebooks with impressions, emotions and other people's stories. I've been sawn in half on live television (still don't know how the magician did it), was one of the first women to wear a mini-skirt on BBC Television in the Sixties (a little bottle-green Mary Quant number), and was also one of the first women to have a late night current affairs BBC TV programme (so late that I don't think many people watched it).

I am the host of South Africa's longest-running radio talk show with the same host, *Believe it Or Not*, which is broadcast live every Sunday on Radio 702 and 567 Cape Talk. We subtitle the programme *The Way You Choose To Live Your Life* and we talk about ethics and morals, faith and religion, spiritual paths and things that go bump in the night. The programme has listeners all over the world – the marvels of the Net – in Alaska, London, Hawaii and Berlin, Perth, Peru and Pofadder. I get hundreds of emails, faxes and letters on a regular basis from people wanting to know more about a particular topic or person, and sometimes even telephone calls in the middle of the night. In over eleven years of the programme's existence I have never done a pre-recording or taped an interview. Everything you hear or have heard is real time and happening 'now'.

I've spoken to people who have seen apparitions – of the Virgin Mary, of a bleeding chalice, of a Hindu god sipping milk, of a departed loved one. And lots of people who've seen, spoken to, or been guided by angels. I've interviewed shamans and sanusis, traditional healers and medicine men. I've found out about reiki and reflexology, holotropic breathing and Zen therapy, past life regression and therapeutic hypnosis, watched the laying on of hands and had a personal, quite wonderful, transcendental experience. I've listened to pagans and pantheists, past and present drug addicts and people with terminal illnesses. And people who have recovered from terminal illnesses. I've heard Buddhist bells, Hindu chants, Hare Krishna incantations and Aboriginal didgeridoos. I've listened to the sounds of Native American and Gregorian chants, voices from psychics and people speaking in tongues. I've tasted sacred plant medicines, eaten mopane worms in the Kalahari and witchity grubs outside Alice Springs and tried to come to grips with quantum physics and Superstring theories.

I've been to many of the world's great sacred and spiritual sites – Machu Picchu, Lake Titicaca's Island of the Sun, Stonehenge, Cambodia's Angkor Wat, Ayer's Rock (now called by its Aboriginal name, Uluru), the Pyramids of Giza, the Bramaputra River in Tibet and the Taj Mahal. (Yes, the Taj Mahal is a spiritual site, celebrating the spirit of human love.) I've stood in awe at the great cathedrals of the world – Canterbury Cathedral, Notre Dame in Paris, that mighty awe-inspiring Gothic cathedral in Cologne, and gazed in wonder at the beautiful 'White Rose of the Desert', a small chapel in Arizona's red desert, and at the tiny 'cathedral' of Pella in South Africa's Northern Cape province, built by a French priest from drawings in an encyclopaedia.

There are so many places of worship – great and small – all over the world. I've stood in the huge cool vaulted interior of

Istanbul's Hagia Sophia, and a short walk away watched a Whirling Dervish spin himself into a trance under the great dome of the Blue Mosque. I've waited in the courtyard of the world's third largest mosque – Hassan II in Casablanca, where 80 000 worshippers can all pray at the same time – and watched the sun glint off the golden dome of one of Islam's most sacred places – the spectacular Dome of the Rock in Jerusalem, whence the Prophet Mohammed is believed to have ascended to heaven. I've gazed at hairs from the beard of the Prophet and at the Dalai Lama's tiny tricycle in his Summer Palace in Tibet. I've also watched and waited at Calvary and marvelled at how a small number of Jews held out against the mighty Roman Empire at Masada, also in Israel. I've shivered in Moscow's Red Square, not from cold, but in awe at the magnificent Cathedral of St Basil. I've heard the bells tinkling and the monks praying in a Jain temple in India's north-west province of Rajasthan, and sat cross-legged with chanting monks in Tibet's most holy temple, Jokang in Lhasa. And at Pashupathinath, the ancient Hindu temple in Kathmandu, Nepal, I've sat beside the saddhus – holy men who have never cut their hair. I've climbed part of the Great Wall of China, wandered in Beijing's Forbidden City, heard the stars sing in the Kalahari, ridden on a camel over the golden dunes of the Sahara and watched the great whales breach and blow in Antarctica.

And so, my life has been full of promise and fulfilment. It's not always been a smooth road that I've travelled – literally and metaphorically – indeed, often a rocky one, and many times I've taken the road less travelled. But I always set out with hope and joy in my heart, determined to 'Have A Go!' It's been a journey of happiness and some sadness, but at its heart my journey has always had a spiritual core, a search for something beyond, below and above the surface world.

So come with me . . .

A few years ago I found myself in Tibet with a small group of people. Tibet is the dream destination of many people, especially those who are looking for something beyond the ordinary, who feel irresistibly and spiritually drawn to the mighty peaks and wide valleys of the Himalayas and to the kind, calm people who practise their own gentle, compassionate form of Buddhism there. It's the former home of the Dalai Lama, one of the world's most loved, loving and admired men; it's the subject of spellbinding books and an object of mystery. Who has not heard of Heinrich Harrer's account of his *Seven Years in Tibet,* or heard about the legendary valley of Shangri-la, hidden somewhere among the highest mountains in the world, where humans live in peace and harmony and ageing is unknown?

The people I am with have come together especially for this Tibetan journey. An IT specialist, a mining magnate, an architect, a geologist, a couple of housewives, an estate agent and several others – people from different backgrounds but all with the same agenda, to find out more about this fascinating and still little-known country and maybe, in the course of this journey, to find out more about ourselves too. Three lives will be changed for ever.

Kathmandu Airport is hot and small. As we progress very slowly from waiting line to waiting line in front of Nepalese officials stamping our passports and visas and whatever else they can find to stamp, my Japanese-American friend Gail comes running across the tiled floor between the backpackers and the large American tourist group to greet me. We throw our arms around each other in a huge hug. We have met only once before, on South Africa's north coast in Maputaland, where one long, balmy, starry night we connected deeply and irrevocably as we watched a giant leatherback turtle weighing at least a ton drag herself up from the sea, dig a deep hole and lay her eggs. It was a poignant and memorable spiritual experience that bonded us for ever – I'll tell you about it later.

We are sisters now. A year has passed and we have arranged to meet in Kathmandu and travel to Tibet together. Gail is small, slim and feisty with flashing dark eyes and thick black hair. She travels lighter – in luggage terms – than anybody else I have ever met, carrying only a small duffel bag that I call her 'magic' bag because out of it she produces not only clothes for every occasion, but also goodies for the locals. It's a cornucopia of packets of sweets, bundles of pens and pencils, and once, when we were in Cuba together, packets containing soap, toothpaste, body cream and shampoo, great luxuries in the island that time has frozen for over half a century.

Geographically, culturally and demographically, Nepal is at the crossroads of eastern, central and southern Asia, and is a dynamic amalgam of different cultures. Nepal has thirty-six different ethnic groups and twenty different languages, although Nepalese is the lingua franca. Although Nepal is officially Hindu – the world's only Hindu state – the kingdom has a history of encompassing different religions, cultures and schools of thought. I saw faces whose differences defied description, from the high cheekbones of the mountain tribes to the flat implacable faces of the Hindu mystics, and from the serene smiles of smooth-faced Tibetan monks to grizzled, wrinkled Chinamen.

We drive in a ramshackle bus through the streets of Kathmandu, probably one of the dirtiest places I've ever encountered. Heaps of foul-smelling rotting refuse spill out into the roads. This rubbish is picked at and rummaged in by crows (the ultimate Third World birds), huge pigs and mangy dogs. But paradoxically, for all the filthy litter, this little city has enormous charm with its narrow winding cobbled streets, jumbled squares with tiny interesting shops, corner cafés, overhead terraces and dusty bookshops.

The street life is chaotic and fascinating. Sacred cows with garlands round their necks have right of way and wander through the rain-filled potholes, sublimely (for, after all, they are *sacred* cows) oblivious of the fumes of bus exhaust, or the noise of pounding generators, accelerating Kawasakis and honking trucks. Tourists in drawstring trousers and backpackers brush shoulders with men in sandals, shorts and a variety of T-shirts, and ladies in spotless and brightly coloured saris, like brilliant butterflies. How on earth these immaculately groomed women, with apparently not a splash of mud or mote of dust anywhere on them, have emerged from such squalid surroundings is a mystery. Their long silky scarves are arranged in sartorial perfection and their black hair gleams in the watery sunlight. Some carry matching umbrellas, as if they were off to the Royal Enclosure at Ascot.

Adding to the uncountable throng are snotty-nosed children, young international backpackers, yuppies on their way to Everest, little old wizened men in white dhotis, bicycles and bicycle taxis, ancient buses, ancient trucks, an ancient car or three, creaking carts, and occasionally a leftover American hippie from the Sixties, lounging against a wall, surrounded by the sweet, heady fumes of pot, still trapped in the faded flower power ethos of long ago.

'Hey, don't you love Tibet?' one calls out to us. 'I could stay here for the rest of my life.'

Gail can't help herself. She gives him a withering look.

'This is Nepal. Kathmandu is in Nepal, not Tibet.'

He gives *her* a look that says, *Huh. Wow.*

The next day we visit the Monkey Temple – Swayambhunath – which is perched on a hill overlooking the Kathmandu Valley. As we drive round the walls at the foot of the steps leading up to the complex of sacred buildings, it seems as if they are pitted with a never-ending series of narrow alcoves lined with thousands of prayer wheels. Around these walls, and always in a clockwise direction, the devout walk, spinning the wheels as they pass. It's believed that the more thousands of prayers you spin as you walk, the quicker you will attain Enlightenment.

We climb up three hundred and fifty steps, passing pilgrims moving up and down, hawkers and step-side stalls and hundreds of monkeys. Brownish-yellow monkeys, big ones, little ones, busy ones, still ones, foraging ones, ones sitting quietly, others like naughty children sliding down the railings that separate the two flights of steps – *Whee!* When we reach the top we are assailed by a vibrant mixture of people, buildings, sights, smells and sounds. A Buddhist temple, a Hindu temple and an Indian stupa are cheek by jowl. People are burning incense and candles – all of them, it seems, bent on some personal spiritual errand. Shops and stalls surround the temples and the place has the feel and look of a medieval marketplace. Dogs pee against walls, pigeons peck for titbits and the ubiquitous Third World bird scavenges in amongst the ruckus.

Bells chime as I gaze out at the smog-covered valley below and the misty mountains beyond. Suddenly there's the noise of a thousand bees as murmuring monks in brightly coloured saffron robes carry past us an old man wearing a red robe and seated on an intricately carved litter. There's a lot of horn blowing. Apparently it is the old monk's birthday and he is having a day out.

'Happy birthday!' waves Gail cheerily as the procession trots past us.

That night we eat in an upstairs café with portraits of the Dalai Lama and Jim Morrison on the walls. We choose between Chinese dumplings, chicken fajitas, a Dagwood sandwich and borscht.

The next day in Kathmandu we learn something about death. We visit the famous Hindu pilgrimage site of Pashupathinath and its ghats – where the Hindus burn their dead. A muddy brown river divides the bank where we stand with its temple area, holy men and hawkers, from the opposite bank where there is a hospice for the dying. Triangular-shaped pyres of burning wood as well as ones waiting to be lit are placed at regular intervals along the bank outside the hospice building. The atmosphere is bizarre, alien but not threatening nor creepy in any way.

I have my photograph taken with an impassive saddhu, a holy man clad in an orange tunic layered with decades of dirt. The dried mud on his arm crackles softly against my arm. An old man in a plastic makeshift shelter asks us to sign his petition. He wants monks to be paid instead of having to beg for alms. He has one of the kindest, sweetest faces I have ever seen.

I sit on a low stone wall and look across to the hospice on the opposite bank, maybe the length of a tennis court away. Women in the ubiquitous brightly coloured saris are scattering and arranging flowers and fruit on a smallish stone slab sloping down to the river. When the women turn their backs for a moment, audacious monkeys steal some of the fruit. After the mourners, for that is what they are, are satisfied with their fruit and floral arrangements, they disappear into the white stone hospice building. They emerge a few minutes later with the body of a man who looks older than Methuselah, wrapped in a white cotton shroud. The shroud drops open as they place him on the decorated stone slab. With his ashy grey face and hanging jaw he looks like a caricature of death from a Hieronymus Bosch painting. The women try to straighten his legs but rigor mortis has already set in.

Time seems to stand still. Maybe with our Western sensibilities we should feel shocked, appalled, even fearful perhaps, but we feel none of these things. Three of our group have never seen a dead person before. But it all seems natural and right. Children skip and hop past, passers-by stroll along chatting, dogs lie curled up twitching with dreams in the sun, hawkers punt their wares, the monkeys eat their forbidden fruit. Life goes on. It's a dramatic reminder, a definitive statement, that in the midst of life we are in death. As we walk quietly back along our side of the river, boys are jumping and diving into the muddy water, petals and rubbish float along, and in a single splendid moment of irony, a holy man with floor-length braids takes a picture of a group of American tourists.

'Say cheese!' he exhorts them.

On the opposite bank a body is now burning on a burial ghat – a bonfire of wood and sticks. One white gleaming bone sticks out of the burning embers and there's a sudden 'pop' as another part of the body explodes. Vendors pester us with beads and trinkets and I buy a wooden puppet on a string. There's no doubt about it. In the midst of life we are in death.

'I wouldn't be seen dead in that river,' quips Judy.

I don't know what your personal experience of death is, but in my own experience it can be commonplace yet dignified, as we saw at Pashupathinath, or joyous as when my mother Doris died. It can be a blessed relief, a cruel shock or a quick release, a soft, last, quiet breath. But I believe, and this is what we found out on this particular journey, that it does not have to be terrible, frightening or unnatural. When we set out on our journey to Tibet, we were not looking for death, but we found it, and as a result some of the group lost their fear of it. The ghats at that holy river seemed so natural, so part of the everyday world, so normal. No fuss or ostentation, just simple dignity and acceptance.

But I was soon to have an even closer experience of death.

We've had a long plane journey to get to Kathmandu.

Only the week before, I was sitting with a blind boy and a shaman on the Island of the Sun at Lake Titicaca in Bolivia, regarded by many as one of the most spiritual places in the world. I'd been feeling nauseous and light-headed for a couple of days – to be expected, as we'd been at altitudes of over 14 000 feet for some time.

The shaman, dressed in a multicoloured woven pixie hat and purple tracksuit trousers, studies me deeply as I take my turn to kneel in front of him and place a few flowers at his feet. He is conducting a welcome ceremony for our small group in front of Puma Rock in the middle of the island. He has spent a long time whispering to Ryan, the blind boy. Now it is my turn.

'You are a strong woman and you make other people strong,' he tells me through the interpreter. 'Your work touches many people and will always do so.'

He studies me closely. Suddenly he rummages in the straw bag at his feet and brings out a small glass vial. There are bright-green round pills inside. Their livid colour reminds me of the poisoned cake that Captain Hook baked for Peter Pan.

'Take two of these a day,' he advises me. 'Your sickness will pass.'

And indeed it did.

But now I feel the same symptoms of altitude sickness on my first night in Nepal, only a week after the Bolivian shaman had given me his secret medicine. The green pills have come and gone.

As we walk up the steep narrow street from our hotel in Kathmandu towards the centre of the town, my spaced-out feeling returns. As I try to avoid the rain-filled potholes my breath catches in my throat. I feel as if a giant hand is squeezing my chest. I keep quiet because I don't want to alarm the others. The next day at the pyres of Pashupathinath I feel myself again.

From Kathmandu in Nepal we fly over the mighty Himalayas towards the Forbidden City of Lhasa in Tibet. The familiar shape of Mount Everest – aloof, implacable, breathtakingly beautiful – soars above thick cloud banks. The snow gleams under a bright above-the-clouds sun, and the surrounding peaks radiate such a sense of mystery, wonder and seduction that for the first time I begin to understand why people feel compelled to scale them.

Tibet is already exerting her magic. From the air, peak after peak, valley after valley unfold below us, but it's only when we drive through one of these valleys to Tsetsang, our first resting place in Tibet, that we begin to realise this land's majesty. We drive the 93 kilometres to Lhasa from Gongkhar airport with its rock paintings of gods and the Buddhist anthem *Om mani padme hum* covering the cliffs beside the landing strip. Huge mountains tower on either side of the wide valley, fringed with hundreds of willows, where the awesome fast-moving Bramaputra river – the highest river in the world – flows from its source at Mount Kailash, one of the world's holiest places, to the Indian Ocean.

Tibetan villages, like Tibetans themselves, are charming. Compounds of flat-topped brown, mud-brick houses look like mini medieval castles. Each house has five turrets, one at each corner and one in the middle, representing the five elements of air, space, fire, water and earth. From each turret fluttering prayer flags fly – spiritual messages to the beyond. Beautiful, brightly painted wooden window frames surround deep recessed windows, and everything seems well maintained and cared for with pride.

Slender Tibetan women in embroidered aprons and more soberly dressed men sift barley in the compounds using wooden forks. Lift, turn and toss. Lift, turn and toss. The rhythm is as ancient as the songs they sing as they work. Sheep graze in the rough pastures, cows are tethered in or near the villages, and small brown children wave and smile. Two horsemen astride gaily coloured embroidered saddlecloths trot past on sturdy little mountain ponies, on their way to a local gymkhana. We are awed and often moved by the things we see – some of the world's most spectacular scenery, nomads spinning wool on spindles as they walk or ride, blue poppies, fields of wild flowers, glittering lakes, and ancient shrines and temples.

But it's not only for the awe-inspiring beauty of Tibet that we have come here. We are also here to experience everything we can, from the majesty and poignancy of the Dalai Lama's Winter and Summer Palaces, to the people and villages, tiny hill shrines, medieval forts and monasteries in the countryside.

One evening we walk to Jokang Temple, a few steps away from our small traditional hotel deep in the heart of Lhasa's Tibetan quarter and culturally far removed from the modern city's new glass monoliths built by the Chinese to demonstrate their political and economic might. We join the throngs of Tibetans who circle the Temple endlessly by night and day – there are very few other foreigners. Known to many as the Heart of Tibet, pilgrims come from all over the country to pay homage to *Jowo Sakyamuni*, a statue of Buddha claimed to have been made in his lifetime. Pilgrims, awesome in their concentration, count incessant prayers on their prayer beads and spin small cylinders inscribed with written prayers and filled with paper ones. The pilgrims cast themselves to the ground in homage again and again, in the flickering light of thousands of yak butter lamps, as swirls of incense, murmured chants, beating drums and tinkling bells create an almost palpable atmosphere of devotion and veneration.

We pack into the temple and sit amongst the chanting monks on knee-high benches covered with thick cloths of worn brocade. After several minutes I find the atmosphere oppressive and leave. Later, after the prayers have finished, one of our party, a young recently divorced woman from Pretoria, decides to circle the temple one more time. She chances upon a Buddhist convent, is invited in by the gentle nuns, spends the night with them, and tells us the next morning that her life has been changed. We don't press her for details, but we hear after her return home that she has left her job and that nobody knows her whereabouts.

There are life-changing experiences for two others in our small group. Ultra-sensible and sceptical Robert has a 'vision' at Yamdrok Tso – the magnificent turquoise-blue Scorpion Lake, whilst shy, retiring Lorna finally resolves a personal problem as she stands among the wind-blown prayer flags at the top of the 4974-metre Kamba La Pass. Shoulders squared and eyes steely, she makes a decision that she claims she has never regretted. After twenty-four years of marriage she decides to leave her four children and overbearing husband and start a new life.

Another day we make an hour-long journey across the enormous Tsangpo River in a traditional, flat-bottomed wooden ferry and then jolt along in a truck to the oldest monastery in Tibet, Samye, built in the eighth century by King Trisong Detsen. It was here that Buddhism was formally inaugurated in Tibet. The design of this monastery is a huge *mandala* based on the Buddhist cosmological order – a circular design symbol-ising the universe and humankind's search for completeness and self-unity.

Although badly damaged during the Cultural Revolution, the small temple complex has now been largely restored. Inside it is dark, with rolls upon rolls of yellowed parchment scrolls stacked from floor to ceiling – repositories of so much ancient wisdom and knowledge. It's dark and stuffy as we make our way clockwise round its interior and rats scuttle among the roof-high dusty embroidered hangings.

The smell of the yak butter lamps is overpowering. I go outside and sit on a stone seat. Bells chime noon as a young tonsured monk comes up to me and smilingly offers to share his bowl of thin soup. Greasy lumps of something float on its surface. I politely decline. As I write, I'm wearing a bracelet of wooden beads given to me by another of the monks that day.

One morning outside Tsetang, we climb up to the burial grounds of the ancient kings, Yumbu Lhakang – The Tombs of the Kings – and Tibet's first palace. Alien, to my Eurocentric eyes, Buddha-like statues sit complacently over the underground tomb. Inside it's musty, mouldy and I find it aesthetically unappealing. Again, I'm first outside, and as I stand among the fluttering prayer flags gazing at the distant mountains and valleys stretched out in front of me, a very old lady with as wrinkled and creased a face as I've ever seen, grabs me by the arm. Startled, I pull away, but she beams at me benevolently. She presses something cold into my hand. The size of a golf ball, it is a pink, shining crystal. She chatters to me excitedly and then limps away, disappearing over the brow of the hill beneath the flapping prayer flags.

The rest of the group will go on to visit Tashi Llunpo, the famous monastery town which is the seat of the Panchen Lama, second only to the Dalai Lama in spiritual importance. As they approached Shigatse, they saw golden roofs glinting in the sun before marvelling at a 26-metre-high statue of the Maitreya Buddha, the Future Buddha. Later they strolled through the vibrant marketplace and bought wonderful, special things.

As they headed back towards Nepal, surviving and surmounting three spectacular landslides, they took one of the most remarkable road journeys in the world. At one point they were perched at the edge of the Tibetan plateau with the massive Himalayan range stretched out before them. They abandoned their 4x4s and walked along a breathtaking road of narrow gorges and high cliffs dominated by wedges of massive snow-covered peaks.

My friends finally took leave of our wonderful Tibetan crew and crossed the border back into Nepal where they spent the night at a gracious Nepalese hill station. Back in Kathmandu, they visited the medieval city of Bhaktaphur, a UNESCO cultural World Heritage site. As they roamed through the rambling city watching the craftsmen fashion their terracotta pots and wooden artefacts and furniture, one of the group bought a small carved door frame which now sits proudly above the front door of her Sandton apartment in Johannesburg.

'Every time I walk beneath it I remember Tibet,' Pam reminisces. 'The holy places formal and informal, the temples, shrines, boy monks, nomads, yaks, butter lamps, ancient medical *thankas*, thronging markets, lonely mountain passes, wild flowers, awe-inspiring scenery, an aura of tranquillity and spirituality. It helps me to stay grounded after a long, frustrating day at the office.'

But where was Kate while all this was going on? Why was I not there to marvel at the Scorpion Lake, dodge the landslides and admire the blue poppies?

I had been in Tibet just over a week when the altitude sickness became worse. A constant sharp pain nagged at my heart and my left arm began to tingle and feel numb. At last the symptoms became so alarming that I described them to gentle Jill, the leader of our group, a healer and herbalist as well as a veteran of travel in Tibet. She put me straight to bed in my little room in the Snowland Hotel in the old Tibetan quarter of Lhasa, pumped a canvas camping pillow full of oxygen, placed it under my left arm, stuck the pillow's rubber nozzle up my nose and told me to breathe deeply.

'I'm in the next room with my door ajar,' she told me briskly. 'If you need me just shout.'

It was a long night. At times I felt better, at times I remembered the German woman who had died of altitude sickness in Lhasa just a few weeks before our group arrived. At times I dozed, at others I seemed to be fully alert. I think I drifted in and out of consciousness a few times. My sensible Virgoan nature got the better of me at one point. Still clutching the by now half-empty canvas pillow under my arm, I staggered to my case, got out my notebook, and wrote my dying words to my family. They were brief and succinct and I'm keeping them for another occasion.

Finally I called Jill. We arrived at the Tibetan hospital half an hour later. The Emergency Room was much like ER rooms all over the world – filled with grubby children, miserable people with long faces clutching various parts of their anatomies, coughing adults, a drunk or two, and a man with a knife in his neck. I was laid on a narrow metal table of venerable age beside the man with the knife in his neck. Fountains of blood spurted over my head splattering everything within splattering distance.

'I wonder if they've got AIDS in Tibet?' I remember wondering to myself as I lay in extremis.

Finally, an ECG machine, even more venerable than the trolley I was uncomfortably perched on, was wheeled in by four Tibetan medical students in off-white coats. Their average age appeared to be about fifteen. I was stripped down to my knickers in full view of the interested ER inhabitants, and greased electrodes were fastened to my bare boobs. People, bored with looking at one another while waiting their turn for the doctor, were jolted into alertness by the sight of a bare-breasted foreigner. They ambled over and examined my body. Sick though I was, I nevertheless tried to suck everything in and jut out my breasts. Can't let the side down and all that.

The machine hummed and whirred and spewed out long paper strips of illegible writing. The patients-in-waiting made their way back to the benches whilst the doctor on duty looked at the strips, read them and threw them casually over her shoulder as she moved on to the next strip of graphs and hieroglyphics. Even though I really thought I was dying I couldn't help but see the funny side and began to giggle. The man with the knife in his neck gave me a reproachful glance as he was wheeled away.

Then I too was wheeled out of ER, my trolley squealing and complaining as we passed through seemingly interminable long dark corridors and finally into a small bare ward with no blankets on the bed and a chipped kidney bowl beside it. Jill held my hands and we chatted to take our minds off what was going on. Finally the specialist, summoned from the depths of the hospital to examine me, arrived clutching the long strips of paper.

'I don't understand this,' he said frowning in concentration as he re-examined me. 'But I think you must go home.'

So home I went. It was a frightening journey, alone and sick and not really knowing what was wrong with me. I repeated a self-made mantra under my breath all the way from Lhasa to Kathmandu, and from Singapore to Johannesburg: 'Please God, don't let me die before I get home!'

And once I got home the symptoms disappeared completely. I was admitted to hospital, given a thorough check-up, and pronounced in excellent health.

But I learned a very valuable lesson. I found out that,

although I really believed I was dying, I wasn't frightened. I certainly didn't want to leave my family and friends, but if this was it, why then, this was it.

'I've had a full and fulfilling life, don't have very much unfinished business, have some regrets, but if the time has come, the time has come,' I told myself philosophically.

With these not very profound thoughts, I was quite prepared to shut up shop, pull down the shutters and close the doors of my temporal life. To tell you the real truth, I was even a bit curious about the whole process. This was one journey that would be completely new to me . . .

Some weeks later I met with an old friend, a psychologist, a Lifeline counsellor and a deeply spiritual person. I told her my story. Ida listened gravely.

'Don't you see, Kate, that this was an initiation for you? A rehearsal for when you do finally die? And you've been privileged to learn a very important lesson – that death holds no fear for you.'

So I've found out that I'm not afraid of dying. What they do with my body – whether it gets put on a pyre like those at Pashupathinath, committed to the deep, or burned to ashes and scattered somewhere in the African bush – doesn't really matter.

It's the soul journey that's most important.

3

The Ballroom in Beijing

It's not enough to dream about going on a journey. Yes, of course, we've all been armchair travellers at some time or other, but the day comes when we have to make a start. We must take that first irrevocable step. Otherwise our lives will not change and at the end we could be well be thinking, 'If only . . .'

Sometimes fate or chance gives us a kick-start. As I'm writing this I receive a phone call from Martha who has just arrived in South Africa to visit her daughter. Now synchronicity takes over. Last night she turned on my radio programme and heard Natalie talking about the 800-kilometre, 34-day solitary pilgrimage she had made from south-west France to northern Spain – the El Camino trail that ends in Santiago. It was hard, cruel, frustrating, often tedious, yet fascinating and exciting. But Natalie's sense of achievement as she walked into the Cathedral of Santiago that last morning was overwhelming. She wept as she sat among hundreds of other pilgrims in that sacred place so far from home. Natalie's adventures had us in thrall for an hour.

This morning I can hear the excitement and resolve in Martha's voice as she tells me: 'I've heard about this pilgrimage and always wanted to make it. After hearing Natalie's story, I know now the time has come for me to go. Please put me in touch with Natalie. My mind is made up.'

Martha's moment has come. She has promised to contact me when she returns from her pilgrimage. I have no doubt whatsoever that she will achieve her wish and complete the longed-for, much-read-about journey.

The part that synchronicity plays in all our lives used to amaze me. Not any more. Sometimes, however, we just have to bite the proverbial bullet and embark on a course of action without outside help. And when you've made that decision it so often happens to have been at exactly the right time. But don't put it off too long.

I'm often asked who of all the people I've interviewed over the years I remember best. Who made the greatest impact on me?

That's not easy to answer. I've interviewed some of the world's great celebrities, talked to people from all walks of life, listened to sages, gurus, mystics, cranks and hypocrites. But I do remember one man in particular. He was an Anglican chaplain who counselled dying people. He told me that the saddest thing in his life was the number of people – especially women – who said to him as they died: 'I wish I'd done more with my life.'

It's one of the most poignant remarks I've ever heard.

If you're about to go on a journey, it helps to have a guide. Sometimes we are clearly shown a guide, sometimes not. In my case, my mother Doris was my inspiration and mentor.

Unsurprisingly, her influence continues to inspire others, even to this day.

Shortly after *There's More To Life Than Surface* was published, I received a letter that touched my soul and reduced me to tears. I haven't changed a word . . .

Dear Kate Turkington!

I wept today as I read page 159 of your book, 'There's More To Life Than Surface'. *Not because I am suddenly aware of my own spirituality (although, believe me, your wonderful book is bound to be of significant influence), but because of the death of your beloved sister, Rita. You see, she was headmistress of the boarding school I attended in Bulawayo – St Peter's Diocesan. I knew the first time I ever saw you on TV that you had to be related to 'Mrs MacGregor'. You were so like her. I have often wondered about Rita, her whereabouts and her well-being. Just a few months ago, a dear friend (and sister-in-law) Jane and I – together with her mother, Sonia (Sonia Hattin of broadcasting fame in Rhodesia and a friend of Rita's) – were talking about Rita. I said that I had an Australian address somewhere and would try writing – I didn't get around to it. When I heard your interview on SAFM (about your new book), I thought again how much you reminded me of 'my Mrs MacGregor'! I bought the book a few days ago. I read that your sister's name was Rita and said to myself, 'I knew it!' Then you spoke about your nephew, William – another piece of the puzzle. Further into the book, I thought, hang on, am I over-reacting? You see, I didn't know about her amazing adventures in New Guinea and other connections. I thought she came from England to our school. So, no mention of her having worked in Rhodesia, I began to have doubts. Then – page 156 – Hallelujah! Now there was no doubt. I would write to you and ask for an address.*

But my joy was short-lived. I wept. I wept for that amazing, interesting, kind, funny, warm, generous, beautiful and oh so intelligent woman, about whom I knew so little. But I loved and admired her. She influenced me in the most positive way. I telephoned Jane in Cape Town to tell her what I had just read. Jane and I used to babysit William and his sister Katie. Mrs MacGregor would make sure there was a fire blazing in the hearth on cold winter nights. She would treat us like adults, even giving us a small glass of wine or sherry! Then she would leave for the theatre (to perform in amateur dramatic productions usually). She advised over boyfriends, make-up and clothes. She once organised a date for me for a school dance – Gordon, a Mormon, who was acting in a play opposite her. She taught me A Level English believe it or not! She used to allow me to pop out of her office, where she held these classes for us – six privileged girls – to collect my hand-delivered letters from a boyfriend, a student teacher, who would arrive on his rather loud motorcycle to deposit these missives into the post-box which was just outside her office window!

I knew Rita MacGregor was special, but only now do I realise just how special. I only wish I had kept in touch with her over the years. Her continued influence could only further have enhanced my life.

Only recently, rather late in my life, have I become a mother. I can only imagine the pain that William's mother went through during his drug and alcohol addictions. My little daughter, Julia, is such a bright little thing – so eager to learn and asking questions, wanting to know what the words in her books mean. Both you and Rita have lived such full, meaningful lives. I can't help thinking that must be partly due to your mother's love of books and her free spirit.

One of the best compliments I have received all my life was

41

during my O Level examinations at St Peter's. Mrs MacGregor
told me how impressed she was with an English Literature paper of
mine. Boy, did I feel good! I have never forgotten that when I left
school, Mrs Mac, together with two other wonderful teachers, came
to the Railway Station to bid me farewell. That meant so much. I
remember Mrs MacGregor saying that she knew I would go far.
Well, I feel that I have let her down badly. Academically I have
achieved very little, although my desire to learn is always there.
Maybe I am not too old to read the books I should have read long
ago. I could educate myself while making sure the material is readily
available for Julia.

We live in a place of unsurpassed beauty and tranquillity. When
I walk and climb alone in the mountains, I feel close to . . . God?
Maybe I should make the time to sit quietly and meditate, and hence
begin, or recognise my spiritual journey.

Thank you for your book. Thank you for what it has taught me.
Thank you for bringing your sister back to me. Thank you for
reading this, for your time. We really are hillbillies, Hugh and I –
this trout farm has never seen a computer! I know my writing is not
the easiest to read, but I had to do this. I had to write this letter.

I wish you well on your spiritual journey. I wish you many
more cosmic hugs.
Yours sincerely,
Sue van der Riet

In a way, both Rita and Doris were Sue's guides, as they were
mine. But sometimes you have to do it on your own. Laura was
a person who did just that.

In the early Nineties I found myself in Chicago. I was to deliver
a paper on Cultural Diversity in South Africa and how our

richness of cultures, backgrounds, creeds and races could add value to business organisations. This was a heady, if uncertain, time in South Africa. Nelson Mandela had been released from prison, we were about to embark on our first democratic elections. The glass-half-empty doomsday prophets understandably prophesied doom, death and destruction; the glass-half-full folk (of whom I was one) saw boundless opportunity, exciting challenges and a whole new world. My paper attracted a large audience. I was from South Africa, and although not black (which would have been an added bonus), I was a woman, an academic and South Africa was flavour-of-the-month. Everybody wanted News from the Front.

At the end of the paper, a late-thirtyish woman bounded up to me. Her greeny-brown eyes sparkled, her blonde bob bounced round her shoulders and she exuded energy, determination and positiveness. Laura was CEO of an American company that promoted cultural diversity in the workplace. She had had great success with her work and wanted to ask me about conditions in South Africa. We bonded immediately.

That evening, as we took a boat cruise on Lake Michigan round the Windy City's stunning skyline, she told me about herself. Of Finnish descent, her family had come to the States two generations ago and had settled there happily and successfully. She was one of six children in a warm, close family and was now living and working in Massachusetts.

Laura proved to be an exceptional woman. Two summers before, determined to find out more about her ancestors and her country of origin, she had taken herself off to Finland. There, much to the horror of the more cautious members of her family and friends, she had gone to live in a log cabin deep in a remote Finnish forest. Her only neighbours (who spoke no English) lived some miles away so her immediate friends were the animals of the forest and the strange birds she fed every morning with scraps of leftover food. She told me later (for we became fast friends), that those few solitary weeks became the turning point in her life. During that time she made a major decision that would change her life irrevocably. To this day she believes 'The Universe' led her into that dark, snow-covered forest.

All this I was to find out later when, for the first time, she visited her 'African family' (for that is the name she gave us) and took us into her heart and her confidence. Again, her cautious American friends and family warned her about coming to Africa.

'To Johannesburg? Crime Centre of the World? Are you mad? Do you know what you're doing?'

Of course she did. One night, in a remote bush camp in the far north of the Kruger Park, under a sky so heavily laden with stars that it threatened to engulf us, she told us of her plans. Two of my grandchildren, Matthew and his sister Tessa, whom Laura adored, and who in turn adored her, sat with Alan and me as she poured out her heart.

Some years previously, Laura had met, fallen in love and married the man of her dreams. He was handsome, charming, clever and, although this wouldn't have made any difference to Laura, very rich. There was only one fly in the ointment. Jack's sister had been a US Olympic gold medallist. After the particular Olympics that she had starred in, she felt her worth and importance diminishing, had sunk into a deep depression and committed suicide. Jack was understandably devastated. He told Laura that he loved her, wanted to marry her, and live happily ever after. But on one condition – there would be no children. He believed that a recessive gene motivated suicide ('Look at

44

Ernest Hemingway and his family!' he cited), and therefore didn't want to carry on a line that would be predisposed to suicide.

Like most women, Laura believed she could change him. Young, happy, in love; of course they would have children she told herself. The years went by, Jack's determination grew stronger, and Laura felt more and more frustrated and sad. When she went to her own happy family gatherings and saw the nieces and nephews, granddaughters and grandsons multiplying, her grief deepened. Although she still loved Jack dearly, she decided to divorce him. And made an even more momentous decision. She would adopt a child and become a single parent.

As the sparks of the campfire sizzled and flew, a lion grunted in the distance. We listened to the noises of the night. A Fiery-necked Nightjar called 'Good Lord deliver us!' A hyena whooped. A Scops Owl purred softly. A log fell off the fire with a crackle.

'I've decided to adopt a little girl,' Laura told us.

On that first occasion when I met Laura, my daughter Sarah had been in Chicago with me. Laura and Sarah had also bonded. Now Sarah was a single parent with a little boy of eighteen months. Stephen was a delight to all of us. It hadn't been easy for Sarah – a full-time working mother with a small baby to bring up – but like Laura, Sarah had the support and encouragement of a large, loving family who believed that together they could do it.

'I've been through all the preliminaries,' Laura told us. 'I've been investigated, examined, had social workers in my house watching to see if I'm a suitable adoptive mother, had my finances scrutinised, even my health examined. Even had my mind read! And I've made the grade, I am ready, willing, able and fit to adopt a baby.'

We were delighted with her news and put our arms around her and hugged her. We'd always felt that Laura was one of those women who was meant to be a mother – warm, loving, open, funny, compassionate and wise.

'But wait! There's more!' she added.

The lion called again softly. He was closer now.

'I'm adopting a Chinese baby. I'm waiting for word as to when I go to China to fetch her. And her name is Savannah Long ("Dragon").'

Let Laura take up the story now. This is what she wrote to me:

If I had been able to script it, the story could not have been more perfect. Imagine the President of the United States going to China to deliver an important speech on Human Rights at the same time that I was going to China to get my little daughter! In my wildest dreams, I could never have believed that this would be happening! Yet it was. Tiananmen Square was sparkling with tiny lights in honour of the occasion. As my dear friend Anne and I walked the Square in Beijing we caught the rare sight of the Chinese and United States flags flying side by side in the evening breeze and the miracle began to become real. My soul knew that I had come to the right place, at the right time, and that this was meant to be . . .

The next day we flew to Nanchang in Jiang Xi Province in The People's Republic of China with the other fourteen families in our group. On the way to the airport we were told that plans had been changed and we were getting our babies that night. The feelings of excitement, anticipation and joy that we were all experiencing are almost impossible to describe. In several hours, our lives would be changed for ever. All of us were 'first time' parents, except one, my friend, Anne. Five members, including me, were to be 'Single Moms'.

All of us were from the East Coast of America and all were realising that this dream of adopting a child was about to become true.

'Tell me about your labour,' I said to Anne as we walked around the lake near the hotel, waiting for 5.30pm to arrive.

The hotel staff had already wheeled a little crib into each of our hotel rooms – 15 rooms in a row in our modern atrium-style hotel in rural China. Not unlike a hospital labour ward. Realising that this was my 'labour', it was comforting to hear about Anne's labour with her son, Matthew. It had been a long and difficult one – luckily for me – as it temporarily distracted me from the reality of the moment. All my feelings, joyous and fearful, escalated as time passed and we got closer to 5.30pm.

We soon joined the others who were waiting outside the double elevator doors in the ballroom on the 10th floor. We made light conversation and did a lot of pacing back and forth.

At around 5.30pm, as promised, on June 28th in Nanchang, China, in the ballroom at the Lakeview Hotel, the elevator doors opened and out of the elevator came the most dazzling sight I had ever seen in my entire life. Out walked 15 Chinese nannies with 15 beautiful baby girls. It was like the Miss Universe Pageant – absolutely stunning. A hush came over the parents. It was impossible to tell which child was yours. And they were all so gorgeous. Each child was approximately a year old (their true birth dates were never revealed to us) and each was dressed in a tiny silken cheongsam – the traditional high-collared long dress of Chinese women. Yellow, blue, green, white – but there was one most beautiful little girl in a scarlet one. My heart stopped. I glanced over to her and prayed, 'Dear God, let that one be mine.'

The babies, who had come four hours by bus from Ying Tan, were called by their Chinese names so that their parent or parents could step up and receive them. 'Fu Long' was the call for me to come

for Savannah – the name I had already given her. I held my breath.
Then I walked forward to receive my daughter from the orphanage
directors. The little girl in the scarlet cheongsam was put into my
arms. My heart soared.

I felt ecstatically joyous and overwhelmingly peaceful. After our
long journeys, we were together at last. I was very quiet and gentle
with her as we walked slowly down the hotel passage to our room.
I told her that I knew she had been through a very long day and that
I would feel tired and scared too, just like her. She then put her little
right finger under the strap of my sleeveless dress and softly touched
my shoulder as if to comfort me. We walked quietly forward.
Savannah became very calm and then put her forehead against mine.
And that was it. We were now mother and daughter for the rest of
our lives . . .

We received the official announcement of Savannah's adoption
a few weeks later.

With the greatest of joy
Laura Lee Kangas
And Savannah Long ('Dragon') Kangas
Announce the adoption of each other
As Mother and Daughter
June 28, 1998
Nanchang, Jiang Xi province
The People's Republic of China

Savannah's 1st birthday was celebrated 7/12/98

We are so very grateful for all our blessings

Laura brought Savannah to see her African family when she was two and a half years old. Although she was still the beautiful child of Laura's dreams, she was also now a true American, with an American accent, American likes and dislikes, patent leather shoes and white socks.

'Let her run around barefoot. She won't catch anything, it won't hurt her,' we told Laura.

In no time at all, Savannah was 'Africanised', playing in the mud, getting delightfully dirty, learning to swim and falling in love with her African 'cousins'.

'You must remember I'm a first-time Mom,' laughed Laura. 'I can't help being overprotective!'

Laura found out that Savannah had spent time in a Buddhist monastery when she was four months old. Even at two and a half, Savannah had an amazing quality of stillness about her. When she heard bells, she sat very still and seemed to gaze into the distance. We took her to the underground hide at Kwa Maritane in the Pilanesburg National Park to watch any game that might come down to drink.

'Sssh!' all the other parents were telling their fidgety kids.

But Savannah sat gazing intently at the waterhole in complete silence, her dark eyes widening as she saw elephants coming to drink.

Although Savannah is now six that quality of calm and tranquillity has never left her. Laura still runs her company and struggles to bring up a daughter as a single parent. But her joy and fulfilment have been so great that they have created another ending to the story.

Laura went back to China two years later and adopted a sister for Savannah called Willow. If you were to see Laura and her two beautiful daughters together your heart would be full of joy.

Just consider, though, if Laura hadn't made up her mind to change her life, those two little girls might still be in a Chinese orphanage, and Laura might have been growing into a lonely, bitter old woman – the kind of woman whose words the Anglican minister had heard so often as he counselled dying people.

'I wish I'd done more with my life . . .'

4

The Princess's Swing

When I was a little girl I used to play at being a princess with my sister Rita. She would sit me on a low over-hanging branch in our wild wood and we would pretend I was on a princess's swing in a palace in some far-off land. Various filmy scarves and pieces of material left over from our mother Doris' dressmaking enterprises were wound round me as I gazed down imperiously at her and our dog Peter. (Peter was the Grand Vizier and always an integral part of our games.)

And years later I find my princess's swing. It is in a Rajah's palace in the legendary north-western province of Rajasthan in India. It was bound to happen one day. As Doris always told us: 'If you want something badly enough, then go get it. It's up to you!'

So I sit on this carved wooden swing not only because of an intrepid mother, but also because of a flinty-hearted, acerbic Mother Superior and the Honourable Gwendolin Fairfax. From them I learned to follow my heart, listen to my head, and not to be afraid of anyone. And just to *do* it.

It has taken me years to recognise the people who pointed out my path. In retrospect, I can see now that it was pretty obvious. However, at the time I was busy loving them, laughing at them, ignoring them, admiring them, putting them on a pedestal or being frightened of them. But it's always worth re-examining the past in order to understand the present or to map the future.

I was educated at Loreto College in St Albans, Hertfordshire. My mother, so keen and hungry for education herself, was determined that my sister Rita and I would have the education that circumstances had denied her. After our six months of forced evacuation in the wet, flat fenlands of England, we came home to a new little semi-detached house in Firwood Avenue, where the rent was £1 per week, a wild wood began where our back garden stopped, and my mother used to rush out (to Rita's and my eternal shame) and gather the droppings of the milkman's horse because they were good for her prized rose garden. Doris had determined that we were now to be made 'ladies' and to be given the best education that Doris and Dick's combined income could buy.

On the very first day at my new school I had a meteoric rise in my fledgling scholastic career. Because I could read so well (I'd been reading and writing fluently since I was four years old), I was immediately promoted to a class two years higher than my own age group. In some ways, this proved an asset. I wrote my matriculation at fourteen, my A Levels at sixteen, took a year off and still went up to university when I was only seventeen. So I got a head start on most of my contemporaries.

The downside of this was that in some subjects – chiefly maths and science – I not only lagged behind the rest of the class, but also most of the time I hadn't a clue what was going on. I never understood why I had to fathom out the speed at which two trains were rushing towards one another (it was dangerous anyway, my practical mind told me), and if I had to find out how long it took for so many men to dig a ditch in so many days, well, I always ended up with half a man in the equation.

This incomprehensible behaviour was interpreted by the Loreto nuns as cavalier in the extreme. How could I get such high marks in the Arts subjects and be so dumb with numbers? She's just not trying. Not true. I really did try but to no avail. Johan Frederick Ahlquist, my Swedish grandfather, erstwhile captain of sailing ships, taught me logarithms and I enjoyed that. Learning logs is embedded in my mind with tales of Captain Ahlquist being becalmed in the Sargasso Sea, of jumping ship and trekking across the frozen wastes of Canada, of his toes being nibbled off by a cruising shark.

I would go up to his little box of a bedroom in Firwood Avenue that was stuffed with souvenirs and mementoes of those days when, according to him, 'The ships were made of wood and the men were made of iron. Not like today, Kate. Now the ships are made of iron, and the men of wood.'

There, watched by a pale ivory Buddha who sat on the old carved oak dressing table, and whose head swung at the slightest movement, out would come the tattered, sea-stained long, narrow log books, and Grandfather Ahlquist would explain their perfect logic. I was ten when he died. Like so many of us, I wish I had listened harder, learned more, written down some of his amazing stories. He spoke several languages, and I have a clear memory of a snowy Christmas Eve, not long before he died, when a party of Russian sailors somehow made their way to Grandfather in Firwood Avenue. Bottles of vodka (how exotic!)

were produced, tongues loosened, and in no time at all, my grandfather was speaking fluent Russian and singing Russian drinking songs.

Learning logs, however, proved to be the pinnacle of my mathematical achievements. Oh yes, I learned all the theorems in geometry off by heart, which finally got me through matric maths along with the logs. But to this day I believe that if I hadn't been so terrified of my maths teacher – who pursued me relentlessly through my high school years like a hooded avenging fury – I might today be able to fill in my tax forms with some degree of correctness.

It was the Mother Superior Herself who was the maths teacher.

In those days there was a strict hierarchy in the Loreto Order. Those who were well educated, of good family and who brought a good dowry into the order were the 'Mothers'. There were Mother Columba, Mother Gonzaga, Mother Joseph Dolours, Mother Annunciata, Mother Gertrude, Mother This and Mother That, and of course, the Mother Superior Herself. The nuns who came from a poor uneducated background were the 'Sisters' and they did the cooking, sweeping, cleaning and waiting on table. There was a long polished corridor leading past the parquet-floored library and beautiful little chapel and there always seemed to be a sister sweeping this corridor. No matter what time of the day or evening one walked along that corridor ('Never run, girls! Walk! Ladies do not run!'), one would always find a sister with her long black habit hitched up round her waist throwing down used tea leaves from a tin and then sweeping them up. The tea leaves trapped the dust. Tidy mounds of dust and tea leaves with dust motes dancing in the sun above them appeared at regular intervals along the long narrow-windowed corridor like so many mini termite mounds. Nowadays the caste system of the nuns – for that is what it was – seems very elitist and politically incorrect, but that was the way of our school world in the Forties and Fifties.

Mother Columba was the headmistress. A large, imposing woman with a red face, we stood in awe of her, but couldn't help noticing the twinkle in her eye sometimes, when she had to reprimand us for some schoolgirl misdemeanour. I was once hauled up before her for sitting on the hockey field gate with my legs crossed. Ladies never sat with their legs crossed. (Oh, dear Mother Columba, what a blessing you are not alive today!) I pointed out that my legs were only crossed at the ankles.

'It's the principle, Kathleen Wood,' she admonished me. 'Never relax your principles.' But she put a motherly arm round me as she sent me back to class.

On another occasion, with great daring, I cut a bang, or fringe, across my forehead. This time it was Mother Gonzaga, the deputy head, who ordered me up on the stage at morning assembly before the whole school.

'Kathleen Wood, you look like a Hottentot!' I was informed.

I caught Mother Columba's eye and it definitely twinkled.

But vanity of any sort was severely frowned upon. I bought a henna rinse for my long dark hair. As I stood in choir practice, the rays of sunshine filtering through the assembly hall windows turned my pigtails a fiery red.

Mother Gonzaga again. 'Kathleen Wood, you're as bold as brass!'

But I exacted a sweet revenge. I don't think the expression 'emotional blackmail' had been coined back in the Forties, but I was a natural practitioner.

I sang in the school choir and took private singing lessons

with Miss Griffin, the Loreto College singing teacher who wore a wig. My mother offered Rita and me the choice of private singing or private piano lessons. Doris herself was a very good pianist with a natural ear. She could play anything from a bawdy ballad to a Chopin nocturne.

We both chose singing lessons. Not so much practice. At the end of the year, there was always a school concert. At Miss Griffin's suggestion, I learned to sing the sentimental but lovely Irish ballad, 'Mother McCree'. I practised it with Doris at the piano every night. Then I had a stroke of pure genius. I've always been a good mimic so I decided to sing Mother McCree in the strongest Irish accent I could muster. The majority of the nuns were from Ireland. The assembly hall was packed with girls and all the nuns – even the sisters were allowed to attend the end-of-year concert. My girlish voice rang out innocent and pure as I milked the emotional words of the song for all they were worth.

'May God bless you and keep you . . . Mother McCree . . .'

There wasn't a dry eye in the house. Except, of course, for Mother Superior who saw through me with the usual glacial expression in her narrowed pale blue eyes. My best friend Vicki (who was a maths star and therefore not entirely objective) wondered if Mother Superior was a saint. That would explain why she was so ethereal, unapproachable and distant. My mind toyed with this sanctity concept but couldn't buy it. Surely saints were fairly decent human beings. Even though they all seemed to be singularly lacking in a sense of humour.

Vicki and I had bonded when we were very small girls. And we complemented each other perfectly. She was a neat, immaculately groomed little girl with tidily brushed short brown hair and clean socks who moved with purpose. I was untidy, pigtailed, and always rushed everywhere. When I stayed overnight with Vicki, her mother Mildred, a wonderful cook, would make us get up early in the morning so she could clean the bedroom and get breakfast over. But what a breakfast! The Smiths had a waffle machine – an unheard of device in post-war Britain and Mildred made the best golden crispy waffles in the world. And Jack, Vicki's Dad, who had spent five years in India during the war, was one of the first people to have a television set. A television set! But he would become very annoyed with me when I criticised some of the programmes with all the intellectual arrogance of a precocious teenager. He would quell my comments with a look, while Vicki and I giggled behind his back. But I knew instinctively that he always admired my spirit. Life at Vicki's was ordered, ordained and secure.

Doris, on the other hand, when Vicki stayed over at our house, urged us to stay in bed in the mornings as long as we wanted. She was happy to have us 'out of the way'. Doris was also the worst cook in the world. She once made pancakes on Pancake Day, Shrove Tuesday, and, thrilled with her culinary prowess, triumphantly and gaily tossed them high into the air. They stuck to the kitchen ceiling and my father had to get them down with a broom. And we had no television. But we played games, card games, word games, and sang round the piano at night. But what Vicki and I had in common, and still do to this day, was a shared curiosity about life and a highly developed sense of humour. We laughed at the world together.

We decided to join the Girl Guides. Our Guide Mistress, another The Honourable, this time the Hon Celia, was tall, imposing, bulky and very aristocratic. She didn't take to us because we were not really her idea of ladies-to-be, were not compliant acolytes, and besides we laughed at her behind her back.

Our troop met in the grounds of a stately old home with a lake fringed by reeds and old trees, where beautifully groomed ducks paddled confidently as we sang our Girl Guide songs in the gathering twilight. But a serpent lurked in this pastoral paradise. The Hon Celia had an ancient, fat, smelly dog named Sammy. She doted upon Sammy with all the pent-up passion of a frustrated spinster. (This was our considered interpretation of her devotion.) Sammy, who was some kind of pedigreed black spaniel, had the unfortunate habit of waddling into the lake (the ducks ignored him) and then choosing somebody to come and shake himself all over before subsiding heavily with his head on a lap. Of course, it was always Vicki's or my lap. It was impossible to hide our feelings, and the Hon Celia's dislike of us was fuelled on a weekly basis. The smell of an old, wet dog with bad breath and bowel problems became inextricably linked with Lord Baden-Powell, long halcyon summer evenings, woods full of bluebells, Be Prepared, and starched blue uniforms with lots of merit badges on our long sleeves. Oh yes, we achieved lots of badges to spite, or even in spite of, the Hon Celia. To this day I can tie a sheetbend and a sheepshank knot, fry an egg over a hot stone, navigate by the stars, box the compass and light a fire with three matches in a howling gale with one hand tied behind my back.

And so I continued to ricochet between the unyielding barriers of the Mother Superior and the Hon Celia. But other human traps lay in wait.

Forgetting one's needlework for the embroidery teacher Miss Tait, another archetypal dried-up old spinster, was a crime to be reported immediately to the Mother Superior. One day, when I was about thirteen, I left my needlework at home. I was embroidering a tray cloth of very complicated design (I still have that tray cloth) and in my rush not to miss the bus for school I had left it behind. Miss Tait, a devoted acolyte of the Mother Superior, glowered and said she would have to report me.

'But I've finished it!' I exclaimed in panic.

She looked at me warily. 'Very well,' she said reluctantly, 'if you bring it in tomorrow, I will make allowances for your irresponsibility.'

All this for a tray cloth!

When I got home from school that afternoon I burst into tears as I told my mother and Rita what I had said.

'It's not even a quarter finished,' I sobbed. 'What will I do?'

Doris as always rose to the occasion. 'Don't worry,' she said briskly. 'Go and do your homework. Rita and I will finish embroidering your tray cloth tonight.'

And finish it they did, sitting up half the night sewing backstitch, lazy-daisy stitch, satin stitch, chain stitch and cross-stitch. When I handed it in triumphantly to Miss Tait the next day – 'I told you I'd finished it!' – a look of profound disappointment crossed her thin face. She examined the back of the cloth and pronounced it untidy.

'In future, always darn the ends of your embroidery threads in.'

And so the matter was closed.

But the episode taught me a couple of things. That to have family to depend on in times of trouble is one of the greatest of all blessings. Secondly, as my mother and sister sat up stitching and clipping for all those long hours, I saw that in reality, nobody had the power to harm me. I would have got a tongue-lashing from Miss Tait, and another much worse one from the MS.

But so what?

Life would go on and would be what I made of it. Let withering scorn and heated coals and all that stuff be heaped on me. It wouldn't really make a difference to me. Life was something to be faced, not run away from. At the time it was a seemingly insignificant incident but one that taught me a huge life lesson.

Never before or since have I been so frightened of anybody. My husband says that because I'm not frightened of anything I have no imagination. But the Mother Superior frightened me. It wasn't just her icy, intimidating manner, her caustic tongue and her overall coldness; it was as if there was nothing in her I could respond to. She was probably the most distant, austere and acidic person I have ever known.

Later, when I taught English literature at university, I was able to see her as one of Ben Jonson's Humours – Bile. She took pleasure in goading and baiting me, knowing that I didn't or couldn't understand the maths she was trying to teach me.

And I knew she resented me in some way. Was it my high spirits, my cleverness, my lust for life, my energy, my youth? All that promise? Now I could put a hundred pop psychology reasons to her dislike, but then I merely labelled her The Ice Maiden. When I finally won an Open University Scholarship she could hardly bring herself to congratulate me. Her look said, 'You'll never come to any good.'

In a last talk with our small sixth form of only five girls, all of us eager and ready to leave school and face the big, bad world, she gave us this immortal advice: 'Your lives are like plastic bowls, make sure they are moulded in the right way.'

And without drawing breath, 'Never wear low-cut dresses. They inflame men's passions.'

Vicki and I rushed out immediately and bought low-cut dresses. Mine wasn't actually a dress, but a scarlet velvet off-the-shoulder blouse that I wore to great effect at my first university 'hop'. (And boy, was she right!)

What did I learn from Mother Superior? I learned never again to be really frightened of anybody. Because nobody is worth that kind of fear. It's as if all my latent fear got used up with her.

My life, and that of my best friend Vicki, was changed for ever by the arrival of the Honourable Gwendolin Fairfax. Fresh down from Oxford, a peer of Kenneth Tynan and other literary glitterati, she swept into Loreto College like a princess. Instead of the usual parade of Irish teachers whose accents we had mocked as they taught us Shakespeare, Milton and Charles Lamb, here was a living, breathing, charismatic young woman who carried us all away with her enthusiasm and charm. And she was English – as befitted a teacher of English Language and Literature. Not bog Irish. (We were tough xenophobes.)

Tall, willowy and blonde, the Hon Gwen, as we came to call her, was the scion of a famous English Catholic family. This was her first job after university and we were her first pupils. Sixteen of us to begin with in the matric class, but just five of us by the time we reached the sixth form. She taught us how to do The Daily Telegraph cryptic crossword. She taught us how to critique live theatre. She taught us how to be worldly. She taught us how to be sophisticated. She taught us how to walk, talk and not be afraid to give our intellectual opinions. She was liberated, like Doris, before the term Women's Lib was ever minted. Once – we held our breath – she even brought the famous theatre critic Tynan to talk to us. He wore a long black overcoat and a black fedora and smoked a cheroot. So-o glamorous.

We worshipped the Hon Gwen. She could do no wrong. She was twenty-two years old and was one of my great formative influences. I was so lucky that she came into my life at the time when I needed a role model other than Doris. It was because of her that I decided to go to university. My heart had been set on treading the boards, and although I gained admission to the Prep Royal Academy of Dramatic Art at the age of fourteen, there was no money for fees.

But the stage was my great and first love. Vicki and I saved up our pocket money, and in the glorious days of the London Theatre, the early Fifties, we saw every production of note that London could offer. Our parents gave us money for food on the days we took the steam train to London, but we ate nothing and rather spent the extra money on good seats. The 'gods' were all right for the hoi polloi but not for serious theatregoers like ourselves. We saw Danny Kaye (who saw us standing at the back of the stalls because the performance was sold out, and who personally called us to come and sit in two unoccupied front seats). We saw Howard Keel, Mary Martin and Sean Connery (who was in the chorus line and who nobody knew at the time) in 'South Pacific'. We saw 'Oklahoma', 'Annie Get Your Gun', 'Kismet' and 'Kiss Me Kate'. We ogled over Tyrone Power in 'Mr Roberts', Paul Schofield in 'Ring Round the Moon', Donald Wolfit as Tamburlaine, John Gielgud as Hamlet and Richard Burton as Romeo. We saw T S Eliot's 'Murder in the Cathedral' and pretended to understand every word.

When the Hon Gwen came into our lives she joined our outings to the London theatre. With her, Vicki and I watched Orson Welles play Othello on the London stage. I turned to her at the interval and remarked, starry-eyed, that it seemed to me that every time he came on stage, it lit up. My eyes were glazed with wonder.

'Silly girl!' the Hon Gwen responded tartly. 'The stage did light up! Look at how the lights are positioned!'

It was in that production that the late Peter Finch (oh, but he was gorgeous!) first played the London stage. Brought from Australia by the Oliviers, (and in those days nobody knew about the affair between him and Vivien Leigh), Finch played Iago – a brilliant, dashing performance that started him on his critically acclaimed acting career. He was nearly as good as Orson Welles, glowering jealously behind fretted Moorish screens in built-up boots.

The Hon Gwen polished us. She taught us to take nothing at face value, to be cynical, to be open, to be critical. She opened our eyes to Virginia Woolf, James Jones, Norman Mailer and Colette. We saw her slightly off kilter only once. The Hon Gwen, Vicki and I had been to see a matinée performance of Shaw's 'Caesar and Cleopatra' in London's West End, followed by an evening performance of Shakespeare's 'Antony and Cleopatra'. Laurence Olivier and his wife, Vivien Leigh, were starring in both plays. We were delighted and thrilled with the performances but now critically attuned enough to know that Vivien Leigh made a brilliant kittenish young Cleopatra in the Shaw play, but did not have quite the stature or the voice for the more mature Shakespearian heroine. Conversely, Olivier was much too young and sexy to play Shaw's ageing Julius Caesar, but was divinely credible as the heroic Mark Antony. He took a long time to die though. Discovering Cleopatra seemingly dead (the asp came later), he fell on his sword, deeming life not worth living without her. But it seemed to our newly awakened critical judgements that he fell around too much, gasped too much, rolled about centre stage too much, before finally expiring with a mighty gasp.

But we stood at the stage door anyway later that night and waited for autographs. Vivien Leigh, Scarlett O'Hara herself, came out first, fragile, dainty, obviously tired, but gracious enough to sign our autograph books. Laurence Olivier followed her, and turned the most brilliant, dazzling pair of blue eyes on us that I have ever seen. He was wearing a camelhair overcoat. He stepped towards the Hon Gwen, took her hand in his, raised it to his lips, and kissed it. She blushed crimson, whispered something faintly, and froze to the spot. I suppose being kissed by one of the most famous actors in the world would turn anybody's head. But it reminded us that the Hon Gwen was really only a girl like us. Older yes, and wiser, and certainly more sophisticated, but her feet were made of clay after all.

And it's thanks to all of them – Doris, Mother Superior and the Hon Gwen – that I found the Princess's swing in the Rajah's palace.

India had always fascinated me. Alan's parents had been part of the last days of the British Raj in India in the British Army in the Twenties, and his mother's stories of houseboats in Kashmir, riding up into the hills with the subalterns, and picnicking at dawn at the Taj Mahal rekindled my early enthusiasm for Kipling, and brought sensations of heat and dust. Vicki's father had served in India in World War II and returned with yet more colourful stories. But somehow I had never got round to visiting.

Then, just a few years ago, I picked up a travel brochure in my dentist's waiting room. As the drill whined in the surgery and people waited uncomfortably for their turn in the chair, I read that for one glorious week it was possible to roll back the pages of history, to lift the curtain of time and recapture in royal style the heady excitement, the pomp and pageantry, the quality of a bygone era by embarking on the journey of a lifetime – aboard India's Palace On Wheels. This is the train that takes you to the fabled north-western province of Rajasthan – a wild, romantic area which resonates with images of romance, chivalry, savagery, poetry, and the continuous cycle of love and loss, victory and defeat.

I managed to get together a group of seventeen like-minded people, and so it was that we finally found ourselves garlanded with flowers, greeted by colourfully clad musicians playing the shenai, and welcomed aboard the Palace on Wheels after our plane journey to Delhi via Mumbai.

Now, I could tell you about the gold-embossed carriages, each named after an Indian state with four twin-bedded compartments and a saloon lounge; the ornate ceilings with motifs in green and gold; the original paintings from Rajasthan; the carved wooden headboards; the silk and brocade bedspreads and curtains, the wooden panelling, the bone china, silver and crystal, the superb food, the ever-vigilant, old-world courtesy of our personal attendants Nikunj and Yatendra, dressed in ethnic Rajasthani attire – but there's so much more to tell. So let me try, because India drenches the senses.

After clackety-clacking through the dense, dark Indian night, the train arrives the first morning at the Pink City of Jaipur, rose-red and half as old as time. We're on the eastern fringes of the Thar Desert, an area studded with mountain-top and jungle forts, a-glitter with palaces and pavilions, pleasure domes and temples. I pull back the golden silk curtains beside my bed to see brightly painted elephants, being 'dressed' for the day's activities. Silken scarves are attached to their ears, crimson cloths cover their backs, and blue and gold headdresses complement the white tunics and scarlet turbans of their mahouts. Finally, elephant make-up is applied to cheeks and eyes. Later that day the elephants carry us up over the steep cobbled pathway to the great Amber Fort, some four hundred years old, which majestically overlooks the city from its mountain eyrie. Alan drops his sunglasses. They are gently retrieved by the elephant behind which politely 'hands' them via his trunk to his mahout. Alan then drops his hat. Another elephant picks it up and hands it to him as it passes. Its wise old eyes signal the message, 'Tut, tut. Careless!'

The Maharajah's bedchamber in the heart of the fort is a glittering cocoon. Small, intimate, round, it is adorned with inlays of glass. The attendants close the doors and light oil lamps and this 'glass palace' twinkles like a thousand stars as the flames of the oil lamps flicker, burn and reflect themselves endlessly in the tiny panes of inlaid glass. Those princes of old certainly understood romance. Outside in the long glass hall, windows fashioned of 300-year-old original Venetian glass glow sensuously in the gloom. In the city itself, the pink Hawa Mahal, the 'Palace of the Winds', five storeys high but only one room deep with walls no thicker than 20 centimetres, stands as a delicate sentinel over the streets teeming with life. We wander round Jantar Mantar, the ancient observatory built by a star-gazing prince over three hundred years ago, where the sundial today is only two minutes slow and young couples still come to work out an auspicious wedding date.

The next day the train takes us to the ancient city-fort of Jaisalmer. This sandstone fort with its ninety-nine bastions and four great gates is home to four thousand inhabitants and two small Jain temples where we pull the bell as we enter to signify our respect for the gods. The fort has the feel of a medieval European castle. Eye-catching displays of hand-woven, embroidered cloths hang from the age-old walls. We climb the ramparts and gaze down at the old town and its *havelis* – the exquisitely carved and decorated merchants' houses with their latticed windows, balconies, cupolas and ornate facades of days long gone. If Jaipur is the Pink City, so Jaisalmer is the 'Yellow City' – its buildings of soft yellow sandstone gleaming goldly in the sun.

Later that day we go deep into the desert and ride camels through the soft dunes. Pakistan is only 80 kilometres away. At Jodhpur, the 'Blue City' where the houses are painted Wedgwood blue to withstand the heat of the sun, we lunch at the Umaid Bhawan Palace, a royal residence, part of which is now a hotel. We feel like royalty ourselves.

Early evening we hit a traffic jam. I have never been on the main street of any city in the world with more diverse traffic. Cars, buses, bicycles, tourist buses, elephants, tuk-tuks, bicycle rickshaws, scooters, camels, goats, ancient diesel taxis, monkeys, dogs, pigs, sacred cows and of course, throngs of people.

Another day we visit Udaipur, the city of lakes, palaces, gardens and temples. We cross the lake by boat to the Lake Palace hotel, former summer residence of the Princes of Mewar. The reflections of its white domes and turrets ripple softly in the quiet waters as cross-legged musicians play traditional music to greet us.

Our group achieved four 'Firsts' on the train.

Firstly, we were the first South African group ever to go on the train.

Secondly, I made the first live radio broadcast in the twenty-year history of the Palace on Wheels, when, as we clattered over the open plains, I spoke to John Robbie live on Radio 702 one early evening. I can only imagine the frustration and envy of the people stuck in the Johannesburg rush hour traffic who were listening to my glowing accounts of our right royal journey.

Thirdly, when the train was delayed for a day because of a hold-up on the line, we were taken by bus to a seldom-visited village, Bijaipur, where the handsome Rajah himself, descendant of the great Rajput warrior Shakti Singh and complete with flowing scarlet turban, white jodhpurs and black boots, offered us hospitality at his palace. Fire-eaters and dancers were conjured up to entertain us as we sat under a silken canopy and feasted on local delicacies. (The very potent local drink made *mampoer* seem like heavenly nectar in comparison!)

We climbed the steep stone steps in the palace to explore every nook and cranny and on a tiny terrace facing distant hills I found the Princess's swing. I recalled the Princess's swing of my childhood and pondered the way my life had taken since. How seemingly unrelated incidents, the people who moved in and out of my life, had brought me to this moment. Grandfather Ahlquist, whose sea-stained logs got me through matric; my sister Rita, who fired my imagination and encouraged me to read and read and read, and who made me learn Lady Macbeth's whole sleepwalking scene when I was only eight; the Mother Superior's implacability which taught me resilience; my American friend Laura who reinforced Doris' dictum to pursue your dreams. So many people, so many influences, so many stories.

And now I am in India.

As the sun began to lose its fierce rays we strolled into the village where the villagers had been up all night sweeping and cleaning. We were welcomed into the tiny houses with their cool interiors and greeted like long-lost friends. The village had never before seen such a large group of Westerners. A few of us strayed off and found ourselves in the village school. No desks, no chairs, but children in darned and patched yet spick and span uniforms sprang to their feet as we walked in, their large dark eyes round with astonishment. When, at the schoolmaster's request, they sang the Indian National Anthem for us, I had tears in my eyes as I watched their ardent, young faces.

And what was the fourth 'First'? Perhaps the most magical thing of all. Because of the delay, we were the first group up to that time in the history of the train to see the Taj Mahal by sunrise. Because of the early hour, there was hardly anybody else there. It rose like a fairytale palace from the early morning mist. Built by a bereaved lovesick king for his dead wife, it has to be the most beautiful monument ever conceived. Inside, surrounding the tombs of the king and his queen, are walls decorated with flowers of all kinds – roses, chrysanthemums, jasmine – picked out in semi-precious and precious stones with exquisite delicacy. Indian marble is the best in the world because it is non-porous and translucent. So when you stand in awe inside the gleaming white walls of the Taj Mahal and the sun comes filtering softly through the thick marble walls, it's like being inside a fragile translucent seashell. It's a huge building but as you walk back along the waterway that directs the eye to its startling beauty, the impression of size diminishes. From a hundred metres away, it's as insubstantial as thistledown. You feel as if a puff of air would blow it away.

We had our pictures taken on 'Princess Diana's Bench', where possibly the most poignant photograph ever was taken of her. I had always wanted to be a princess. Not any more.

And the stereotypes of India? Yes, I saw crowds, dirt and poverty as well as riches, splendour and glory, but not despair or hopelessness. Maybe the Hindu doctrines of Karma and Reincarnation teach the people to be gentle and serene.

I shall go back one day.

5

Spine Pads and Outcasts

I graduated with a first class honours degree in English literature when I was twenty-one years old and was offered a graduate scholarship by London University to study for a PhD. It would take two years.

But the summer before, when I was still only twenty, I had met, fallen in love and married Malcolm, who was then finishing his degree in Politics, Philosophy and Economics at Oxford University. When, after a fairytale wedding and a honeymoon spent touring the South of France, I went back to university for my last year, Malcolm flew off to Nigeria where we were to be reunited nine months later. He had accepted the first job that he had been offered on graduation and it was with the United Africa Company. It wasn't so much that he was drawn to Africa (although we both spent most of the rest of our lives there), as because he was offered a £60 kit allowance – a fortune for two students who had been struggling for three years on university grants. And his annual salary seemed huge.

We had to look at a map to find out where Nigeria was. We

heard tales of 'The White Man's Grave', malaria, mosquitoes, jungles, steamy heat and rudimentary accommodation. It didn't deter us one bit. In between Shakespeare, Old Norse and the Metaphysical Poets, I was summoned to Unilever House on the Thames Embankment (UAC was a subsidiary of Unilever) to be interviewed by a be-hatted and be-gloved lady straight out of the pages of a Victorian novel. Over soup, she handed me a lengthy kit list. One item was a spine pad. What on earth was a spine pad? It was like a cricket pad.

'To protect your back from the fatal rays of the sun,' she advised me.

Of course, I didn't buy one, thinking that when this particular lady had lived in Nigeria it must have been the Dark Ages. However, she did give me some good advice, her fuzzy lip trembling with embarrassment as she did so. She lowered her voice to a whisper over her grilled trout: 'No nylon underwear, too hot. Only cotton.'

And so it was that as soon as I had written my Finals, I boarded a BOAC plane (that was what British Airways was called in those days) and took off for Port Harcourt in Nigeria.

Port Harcourt was a sleepy little port in the then Eastern Region of Nigeria. I discovered the wonders of the African market – bright colours, noise, people, animals, fruit and vegetables. Stalls sold everything from reels of cotton to Japanese teddy bears, from rolls and rolls of brightly coloured fabrics to cooking pots and African Penny Dreadfuls. These incredibly romantic, larger-than-life cheap paperbacks comprised the genre now known to scholars of African Literature as Onitsha Market Literature. In my day, they were the Nigerian equivalent of Mills & Boon and eagerly lapped up by the local men and women alike. Chickens with their legs tied together thrashed about on the red clay, and women with their legs stuck straight out in front of them sat on the ground with their hands continuously arranging and rearranging their piles of yams, cassavas and pawpaws on woven mats. Thin dogs scavenged. Large, foul-smelling dried stockfish hung from palm-thatched stalls, and clay pots of palm wine and palm oil marked the boundaries of the market's rabbit warren of alleyways.

Oil had not yet been discovered to change the fate of the country irrevocably and I became part of a typical colonial life of socialising at the Club, playing bridge, dancing and flirting with the numerous young bachelors, giving and going to dinner parties, and learning to play golf. There were lots of eager young men who wanted to get me alone on the sandy golf course with its 'browns' instead of greens and show me how to drive by putting their arms round me and helping me to hold the club.

I resolved to enjoy the life of a colonial madam.

But it was not to be.

News of my academic achievement (I think I was regarded by a lot of the other madams as something of a bluestocking) flashed round the little town and less than three weeks after I had landed at Port Harcourt, I found myself teaching English at a teachers' training college where all the students were Nigerian men who were much older and wiser than I was. From then on, wherever Malcolm was posted (and postings changed very rapidly – I lived in twenty-four different company houses during my first three years in Nigeria), I taught at whatever educational establishments were handy – universities, secondary schools, training colleges, and once as headmistress of a high school in a leper colony. This was at Itu, a tiny trading post on the banks of the Cross River, a hundred miles from the nearest small town of Aba – itself only a dot on the map – and apart from two missionaries and a German doctor at the Itu leper colony, I was the only other European woman for hundreds of miles.

Itu was a strange and exceptional village deep in the heart of Iboland, an area made famous by Chinua Achebe's depiction of it in his landmark novel *Things Fall Apart*. It was a refuge for the *oşu* – the outcasts. An *oşu* was a person dedicated to a god, a thing set apart, a taboo for ever, and his children after him. An *oşu* could not marry a free-born person, and had to live apart from the community, and somehow Itu had become a haven for many of these outcasts. An *oşu* could not attend a ceremony of the free-born, nor go into their houses. The mark of an *oşu*'s forbidden caste was long, tangled, dirty hair, because they were forbidden to cut it or use a razor. When an *oşu* died, he or she was buried apart from the clan in an area known as the Evil Forest. This was also where twins were buried. Twins were considered unnatural and potentially evil and so were killed at birth, crushed into pots and thrown away for leopards to eat. The mother too, was hounded into the bush, where she had to live alone. The mothers were terrified of twin babies and would often kill them themselves if others did not.

On moonlit nights the drums would beat even louder and more powerfully than on other nights as the *oşu* gathered on the river banks below our wooden house on stilts. Strange screams and noises would go on well into the night. Often, when Malcolm was on tour, sometimes for days at a time, I was left alone with the moon, the screams and the drums. But it never occurred to me to be frightened. After all, I was British, and in those days Britannia Ruled the World, and Nigeria was still comfortably pink on the map of the world. Since my experiences with the Mother Superior I had learned not to be frightened of anything or anyone – an attitude I still have today.

Our windows and doors were made of wooden slats and water was brought up from the brown swirling river in buckets. My instruction to Bassey the cook (who had six toes on one foot and sharply filed teeth that gave him the appearance of an amiable vampire when he smiled) when he went to shop for our food in the local market, was always to buy the meat with the skin on. In that way we would know what we were eating. (Mind you, I once ate slices of some delicious meat fried with red peppers and okra, only to find out later that Bassey had stumbled over a dew-bedecked giant land snail one morning, and served that up for supper rather than the more mundane purchases procured on the daily trip to the market.)

In 1957 we celebrated New Year in the great, rambling Itu leper colony church. It was a huge, sprawling, one-storeyed building hand made of red clay with a roof of palm fronds, and was a natural development of the first palm grove where pagan patients and Christian missionaries had first come together to worship in the early days. Every time new space was needed, more red clay was added, more walls were built, the roof was extended and, inside, more red mud pews were added. Now this mathematically impossible structure could hold two and a half thousand people. It was an architectural miracle. Dr and Mrs Macdonald of the Church of Scotland were the missionaries who ran the colony. They were quite unperturbed by this potentially hazardous great natural cathedral, that I believe is standing to this very day. 'It's God's will,' they answered me assuredly when I questioned the stability of the monument.

'Why doesn't it fall down?' I wanted to know.

'Never question the Will of God, dear. Just accept. Always accept God's Will.'

I have written before about this particular New Year when hundreds of lepers were nominated as now 'cleansed'. Their names were called out from the Doctor's lists at midnight on New Year's Eve, which meant that they could now leave the colony and go home. Some of those rejoicing, dancing, singing, 'cleansed' people had been in the leper colony for as long as fifteen years.

I had my first child, 'a beautiful boy' Sister-Doctor Nolan of the Medical Missionaries of Mary told me as she delivered him by gaslight in Anua Hospital. It was the only hospital for hundreds of miles and a two-hour drive over very rough bush roads from the tiny village on the banks of the Cross River where I had spent my pregnancy. Simon was the only white baby and the nuns didn't bother to put an identity band round his tiny wrist. In the room next door, also furnished with a commode and a palm leaf fan, was the First Wife of a very important Ibo Chief. These were the days before scans and ultrasound. Eunice went into labour the day after Simon was born. To her horror she delivered twin sons.

Sister-Matron, who was much more cynical than the other nuns in the order, and who even sneaked a cigarette sometimes as she sat on my bed after her late afternoon rounds, said wearily, 'Those babies will die.'

'What do you mean?' I asked her, horrified.

They were big healthy babies who had weighed in at over seven pounds apiece. The next day Eunice's husband came to fetch her in his old Peugeot. I heard later from the nuns that both babies had 'died'.

Two years and another baby later ('I'm sorry, Madam, it is a female child,' I was told by the sixteen-year-old Nigerian probationer nurse who delivered Sarah), Malcolm and I found ourselves in Calabar, also on the Cross River, an old slaving port of rickety wooden houses, sloping mud streets, a crowded market and steep river banks where the ferry plied its way to and from Itu on a daily basis.

I went to teach at Duke Town Secondary School – four long, low brick buildings with corrugated iron roofs. It was very difficult to make oneself heard when the tropical rains came and drummed on those roofs. The school had about a hundred pupils, boys and girls, and I was the only white teacher.

One day, at the beginning of the rainy season there was a violent electrical storm. I've always loved storms and the elemental strength they represent. Six boys and I were sheltering under the overhanging tin roof outside one of the classrooms. Four of the boys had bare feet, two others were wearing canvas shoes. I was wearing leather sandals. The hot air was still for a moment. Suddenly there was an almighty crack and a bolt of lightning zig-zagged in and out between us. There was a suffocating smell of sulphur as we were blinded by the dazzling white light. When I could see again two boys lay dead on the polished red mud floor. One was at my feet, the other was at the end of the line. Neither had uttered a sound. One was burnt to a cinder, the other looked as if he had lain down and gone peacefully to sleep. One of the dead boys was wearing shoes, the other was not.

That moment will always live with me. But it didn't and doesn't help me to understand if life is really as random as that lightning strike, or if it had been predestined that Moses and Richard would die. And that I would live. Philosophers, writers, poets, priests and theologians have been debating concepts of

Predestination v. Free Will since we first sat in our fur skins hunched over our fires outside our caves. And I firmly believe that nobody has yet come up with a satisfactory answer. Why me? Or why *not* me? have always been two of humankind's central questions. Many traditional religions offer answers, but those answers have never satisfied me.

While we were in Calabar, the old king died. A king or chief was required to be buried with as many followers as possible. Armed men roamed the streets looking for potential grave mates. Bassey locked himself in his room and refused to go to market.

'The king cannot go alone into the spirit world. His followers will kill his family and slaves and anybody else they find in the streets to accompany him on his journey to the next world.'

Rather than being buried alive with the king, Bassey stayed in his room for two weeks and Malcolm and I ate tinned carrots, corned beef, tinned pilchards and Marie biscuits.

Whilst in Eastern Nigeria, we heard of the Long Juju of Arochuku. This was a powerful all-seeing juju that could track down those who offended it and exact dreadful retribution.

I had studied Old Norse at university. Because of Grandfather Johan, and visits to Sweden as a young girl, I had a smattering of Swedish and thought it would be of assistance in reading the Old Norse sagas. Perhaps more importantly, I had inherited all of Rita's university texts. She too was studying English literature and, as part of that course, Old Norse. All her notes and translations were scribbled in the margins of the set works and I became a star at 'unseen' translation in my tutorials. My tutor Mr Ludlum, an earnest young man with a round pimply face and moist fingertips that left a snail-trail when he wrote on the blackboard, was convinced I was some kind of natural genius.

The only other student in my tutorial class was a Nigerian called Sam Okechukwu. In our second year he suddenly vanished. Only years later did I find out what had happened to him. Sam came from a small village not far from Itu. His family and village had put their savings together to send him to an English university following a brilliant secondary school career at Hope Waddell College in Calabar. The village had collectively decided that Sam would study law and ever after be in a position to guide them in matters legal, great or small. This would give them a headstart over neighbouring villages. But Sam, intoxicated by Macbeth and Julius Caesar, Dickens, Kipling, Matthew Arnold and Tennyson, had made up his mind differently. He would study English literature instead.

Somehow the village found out that he had changed his course of study and the village elders went to consult the Long Juju of Arochuku. The Long Juju (so named because it could work across great distances) put a 'face' juju on Sam. He would wake up at night in England sweating and crying, seeing a monstrous face in front of him. This face haunted not only his dreams but also his every waking moment. As he read about Eric the Red discovering Newfoundland, a terrifying African mask danced in front of his eyes, terrorising and mesmerising him. Finally, he was invalided home by the British Council with a 'nervous breakdown'.

Nobody in his right mind messed with the Long Juju of Arochuku. The Aros, keepers of the Juju, were a powerful force in Iboland and a formidable foe. In the old days, they were slave-stealers, seeking their victims everywhere, and selling them in the markets to traders. In Calabar you could still see the old rotting slave posts with their rusting metal hoops where these unfortunate human beings had been chained before being sent off to the New World.

I was once taken to the *chuku* or juju, the Arochuka, which means the God of the Aros. We went by canoe, and then on foot until we arrived at the lip of a rocky gorge. A stream flowed at the bottom of the gorge and there was a deep pool overhung by trees and creepers. Sacred catfish with glittering eyes swam amongst white lilies. It was death to catch these fish. On a tiny island there was a hut guarded by priests, and it was here that the God lived. All of this I was shown and told by a young Catholic priest, Father Pettit, fresh out from Ireland, who believed that by confronting the Juju he could disempower it. The locals listened but ignored his claims that his God was mightier and more terrible than theirs.

I believe that the Long Juju of Arochuku reached out its long arm to me. Many of us have had a particular favourite animal in our lives. That animal is often a dog. One of my most beloved animals ever was a small black French Poodle called Pepé, which Malcolm had bought for me when he left for Nigeria and I stayed alone in England finishing my studies for another nine months.

After I arrived in Port Harcourt from England I sent for Pepé who arrived on a Danish merchant ship. As was the custom on many Scandinavian vessels, the captain's wife sailed with him. Mrs Lundgren begged me to let her keep Pepé. During the six-week voyage she had to come to love him almost as much as I did. But Pepé was not to become an old sea dog. He stayed with me, came to school with me, to the outdoor cinema in the various towns, to the Club . . . and to the Long Juju of Arochuku.

The Aro priests eyed him narrowly. Could they buy him

from me? I think this was the first French Poodle ever to be seen in Iboland. He would surely make powerful juju. Definitely not. I hugged Pepé to me fiercely. During the long canoe journey back to Calabar he whimpered and fidgeted – behaviour that was very out of character. The next day he vanished. In the 1920s, a British military expedition had been sent out to quell and conquer the Long Juju of Arochuku. There was fierce fighting and many lives were lost. But the Long Juju of Arochuku survives to this day. Its long tentacles reached out and took both Sam and my little dog.

One early evening as darkness was creeping over the far river bank and the drums began to beat, I sat with my three-week-old baby son Simon on the rickety wooden veranda of our wooden house on stilts in Itu. A hippo was snorting somewhere below, the village cooking fires were curling up lazily into the hot, sultry air, and a vulture hunkered down noisily in one of the great cottonwood trees surrounding our little patch of garden. I called it a 'garden' because I tried to grow things there like roses and dahlias, but all that grew were Bassey's cassava plants, and hundreds of watery, mushy cucumbers, which were so prolific that at one stage they threatened to engulf the house, like The Quatermass Experiment.

Malcolm was away 'on tour' for a few days visiting trading posts even more remote than Itu. Bassey called me from below the house. I walked down the wooden steps and along the dirt path to the outside kitchen where he produced everything from suet puddings and soggy sweet bread rolls to baked yams and fried peppered slices of snail on a smouldering coal stove. A wizened old man who had paddled his canoe upriver was standing outside the kitchen door holding a small, bedraggled squeaking bunch of feathers. That is how Polly came into my life. She was a very young African Grey parrot and I bought her from the old man for £5 – a fortune in those days. But he fixed me with his glittering eye and I paid up without a murmur. The only sound that Polly could make, other than her natural squeaks and squawks, was to clear her throat and spit – a sound she had learned from her present owner. As the phlegm rattled in his throat as he stood before me, so did Polly imitate him perfectly, and as the greenish globule hit the ground, so Polly's audio globule hit too. It was a class act and one that she never abandoned, saving it for people she didn't like and any passing cat.

Polly became not only part of the family, but also the most marvellous mimic. I never ever knew whether it was the baby crying or Polly having fun. When I called for Bassey, and heard an answering, solemn, 'Madam', I never knew whether it was Polly or Bassey. In later years, when we played bridge, Polly would bid 'Three No Trumps' before I could, and when the table was set for a meal, Polly would jump up and down from one leg to the other shouting in pidgin English, 'Time for Polly's chop! Time for Polly's chop!'

But because I was brought up by a mother who would have us at the railway station an hour before the train was due, 'Better to be safe than sorry!' Doris would declare portentously, and because this same mother kept all the clocks in our house ten minutes fast to 'save time', I have always been paranoic about being late. Malcolm, on the contrary, had no concept of time.

'Hurry up, you'll be late!' I would urge him, when all he had to do was pedal his old bicycle down the river bank to the little tin-roofed trading post where the huge copper palm nut pans glittered in the heat as they lay on the palm 'beaches'.

Although time was of really no importance in the life we led then, I would nevertheless always insist, 'Hurry up, you'll be late!' as if it mattered in this world where the days and months crawled by in a heat haze, the rains came and went, and village life went on as it had done for centuries.

Of course, Polly took this as her rallying cry. 'Hurry up, you'll be late!' she would screech at a passing cockroach, a drifting canoe, or at the most inopportune moment, such as when Mrs Macdonald, wife of the missionary doctor in charge of the Itu leper colony, came to visit in a rare moment of free time. Mrs Macdonald would bring me tins of Dundee cake, sent out by ship from the Macdonalds' loyal parishioners in Scotland and the only food my two-month-old crocodile George would eat. I used to flatten the flap at the back of his throat with the handle of a teaspoon, and push Dundee cake down his gullet.

It was the only food he didn't regurgitate, and he thrived on it. Try him with raw fish, a piece of meat, a lump of cooked cassava – no, he wasn't interested, and out it came. But Dundee cake, that was another matter! He stuck to his saurian guns and only 'did' Dundee cake, and that was that. He lived in a large tin bath, slopping about in the same muddy brown river water that Bassey used to bring up by bucket from the river for my bath.

But George, who had been given to me by the same Ancient Mariner who had brought Polly into our lives, had a much shorter stay. His tiny teeth, which, at two weeks old, were like needles, had become, a few weeks later, razor-sharp and extremely fearsome. Bassey refused to handle him, George was becoming impatient of his tin prison walls and attempting to jail-break, and most important of all, the supplies of Dundee cake were drying up. So George was emptied back into the river and vanished. I swear he gave me a reproachful look as he disappeared into the depths.

As crocodiles live to a very great age, I wonder, as he slithers and slips along the swirling currents of the Cross River, or lies dozing on a muddy river bank in the noonday sun, does he still dream of the halcyon days when he was spoon-fed Dundee cake? Or in the depths of his reptilian consciousness could he ever know that he was possibly the only crocodile in the world to have had such gourmet beginnings?

And Polly? My poor, dear Polly? When I finally left Nigeria and left my husband Malcolm as well, I went to live in Ireland with my new husband, Alan. Alan had been seconded out of the British Army to the Nigerian Army and I fell in love with his Irish accent, his rakish slouch hat with its green feather hackle, and his sun-tanned knees. The move was a major leap of both emotion and faith – from the security of a seven-year marriage to an untried and untested relationship with an almost stranger; from the steamy heat of West Africa to the cold rainy climes of Londonderry in the North of Ireland, where Alan was to be stationed with his regiment.

It was a difficult time for all of us. I was racked with guilt over leaving Malcolm, worried about the children, and wondering whether or not I had done the right thing with my life. I had been given a challenge, faced it, dealt with it, but now didn't know if I had made the right decision. Sometimes Doris' exhortation, 'Have a Go!' seemed to ring a bit hollow in my ears. However, Alan, Simon, Sarah and I settled into a little house in Derry's Bogside. And Polly came too.

After a few months we moved to Bangor, County Down, a small seaside town about half an hour's drive south of Belfast. Polly lived in a large cage in my kitchen and seemed to be happy and well after her long sea journey with us from Africa and a tumultuous crossing over the Irish Sea. She settled in as if she had always lived in cold northern climes and had even learned to swear at the postman. The kitchen was warm, safe and busy and she could look out on the solitary apple tree, the blackcurrant and gooseberry bushes, hurl insults and spit at the local cats, and trade words with a friendly blackbird. She even developed a warm relationship with Miranda, our Irish Beagle, straight from the bogs of Donegal.

One morning there was a knock at the front door. A lugubrious man in overalls with a book under his arm stood there.

'I've come to convert you,' he informed me.

'I don't want to be converted, thank you,' I replied politely.

Word had flashed around the neighbourhood that I was a recently returned Savage from Africa and thus was fair prey for Mormons, Jehovah's Witnesses, Scientologists and other religious groups who came constantly knocking on my door hoping for an instant conversion.

'Oh, no, ma'am,' he said in his beguiling Irish accent, eyes now twinkling, delighted I had been fooled. 'Sure I've come to convert you, but to natural North Sea gas!'

And convert us he did. But North Sea gas is colourless and odourless. One cold winter's day, I put some milk to boil on my newly converted gas stove. And forgot about it. The milk boiled over, extinguished the flame of the gas-ring, but not the gas.

When I finally remembered, there was Polly, flat on her back with her eyes closed, stiff little legs in the air. A dead parrot. It was the end of an era. I just hope that she died dreaming of some long-lost jungle, where other parrots darted and squeaked in amongst the tall trees and the air was charged with the perfume of tropical flowers . . . and where she could hawk and spit to her heart's content. And shout 'Three No Trumps!' to a passing butterfly . . .

Seven years had gone by since I first arrived in Nigeria. Unbeknownst to me, all this time I had been following in the footsteps of a very great and remarkable woman – one who, unlike me, had known from a very early age what she wanted to do, where she wanted to go, and what path she wanted to follow. From Itu to Calabar, from Arochuku to Duke Town, our paths had interconnected and were inextricably entwined. Her name was Mary Slessor.

6

The White Queen of Okoyong

It's important to contextualise Mary's story. She was born at a particular moment in history, at a particular time, in a particular belief system she was prepared to live by and die for. Today parts of her story may seem naïve or politically incorrect, but it is a true story and one that deserves honour and credit. Her integrity and unshakeable faith cannot be denied. I've tried to tell her story through her eyes – a humble Scots girl from early Victorian England.

Mary Slessor was born over 150 years ago in the city of Aberdeen in Scotland. She was the daughter of an alcoholic shoemaker father and a mother who loved to hear stories of faraway lands and people with dark skins and the missionaries who went from the United Presbyterian Church to fight the evils of heathenism.

After church on Sundays, Mrs Slessor would come home with tales of a new mission that had been started amongst a savage race in a wild country called Calabar in West Africa. She would tell Mary and her siblings about the wicked customs the minister had related – including the killing of twin babies and the worship of pagan gods.

In no time at all little Mary was teaching play-school to her dolls whose faces she blacked with coal dust. She resolved to be a missionary herself and work abroad in the service of Jesus. Her brother Robert scoffed at these ideas and reminded her that she was only a girl – girls didn't do this sort of thing in Early Victorian Scotland, particularly if they were poor and un-educated.

But Mary had made up her mind. One day she would become a missionary.

The family moved to Dundee where matters on the home front became so bad that Mrs Slessor and Mary, who was only eleven, were forced to work in the mills and become weavers. At first Mary was only allowed to work for half a day, spending the other half in the factory school where she learned to read and write.

By the time she was fourteen, she had become an expert weaver and was working a large machine. From six in the morning until six at night she worked amidst the whirring machines, whizzing wheels and whirling belts, but she propped a book on a corner of her loom and read whenever she had a moment to spare, and she never lost sight of her dream of going to Darkest Africa.

Unlike the other girls, it was not the popular romantic novels of the day that Mary read but works like Milton's *Paradise Lost* and Carlyle's *Sartor Resartus*. But her favourite book was the Bible. She attended Wishart Church which overlooked the old Port Gate where there always seemed to be rough gangs of boys and girls roaming about swearing and fighting. The young Mary, armed with her Divine Purpose (because that's how she saw her path in life), started teaching at a mission in a little house in Queen Street – the brass inscription commemorating Mary is still there. She tamed many of the unruly youth and brought them to Jesus, often going alone into the dangerous slums where the other teachers would only venture in pairs.

Her dreams never left her. Through the smog, dirt and gloom of the narrow streets she had visions of waving palm trees, a hot tropical sun and tangled jungle. But she was the breadwinner, her mother leant upon her heavily for physical, material and spiritual support, and she was a girl.

How could she fulfil her chosen destiny? She continued to tell herself, 'I *can* do it. I *will* do it.' She was one of the best weavers in the factory and for fourteen long years she took on extra work so she could save money. She began speaking at meetings, and continued to put her faith in her Lord.

Then the news flashed around Dundee: the great Scottish pioneering missionary and explorer David Livingstone had died in a hut in the heart of Africa. This was the sign Mary had been waiting for. She would take up the work of the great pioneer and offer herself as a missionary.

A letter finally arrived from the Mission Board of the United Presbyterian Church in Edinburgh. She tore it open with trembling hands. And then whooped for joy. She had been accepted and was going to Calabar as a teacher.

On an autumn morning in 1876 Mary Slessor stood on the deck of the steamer *Ethiopia* in Liverpool Docks and waved goodbye not only to the two companions who had come to see her off, but also to her previous life.

Weeks later the vessel entered the Calabar River and steamed through waters crowded with strange birds, huge crocodiles and dark mangrove swamps where the roots of the trees seemed to be walking in the water. Mud-skippers, small air-breathing fish, slithered over the river banks, tiny crabs scuttled over the mud flats, and parrots called in the trees.

Duke Town, which was to be her new home, was a huddle of mud huts among the palm trees. High on the same bluff overlooking the river where I would live more than a hundred years later, was the Mission of Daddy and Mammy Anderson, two famous pioneer missionaries.

Calabar was a strange exotic place of rushing waters, steamy heat, strange people, beautiful flowers and shrubs. When I lived there I used to pick Blushing Hibiscus for my dinner parties. If you picked the white blossoms in the early morning and kept them in the gas fridge all day, at night, suitably arranged on the dinner table, they would 'blush' from the palest pink to the deepest crimson as they warmed in the evening heat. At night, I would go out into the garden and fill my lungs with the scent of the moonflowers whose perfume charged the tropical night. They bloomed only after dark, their huge waxy white blossoms gleaming like so many terrestrial stars among the dark green leaves. The next morning they would be dead.

Mary Slessor was a much better missionary than she was a poet, but she wrote about those early days in Calabar with a joy and innocence that speaks to us through the years:

> . . . the shimmering, dancing wavelets
> And the stately, solemn palms,
> The wild, weird chant of the boatmen
> And the natives' evening psalms,
> The noise of myriad insects
> And the firefly's soft bright sheen,

The bush with its thousand terrors
And its never-fading green.

Her innocence and joy, however, were soon to become eroded by the horror of what she found – wild, cruel tribes, slavers, beaten and branded slaves, cannibals, blood and sacrifice. She learned that when a chief died the heads of his wives and slaves were cut off and the bodies buried with him to be his companions in the spirit-land.

She was particularly horrified at the plight of twins. But in order to combat the evils around her she had to be able to communicate with the people. And so she set about learning Efik, the chief language of the area, and so proficient did she become at it that the local people said she was 'blessed with an Efik mouth'.

After three years of arduous, often harrowing work, she got fever so badly that she was sent home to Scotland to recover and recuperate. When she returned to Calabar it was to find that she was to be in charge of the 'Wimmin Work' at Old Town, a place two miles higher up the river and noted for its wickedness.

In Old Town she lived in a mud hut roofed with palm leaves, wore old clothes, went barefoot and ate yam, plantain and fish. But she became a power in the district, allowing the upcountry people to slip through the mission grounds at night with their palm oil, and guiding them past the sentries on the beach to avoid the greedy traders of Calabar who protected their trading rights quite savagely. She began to oppose the custom of killing twins and became known as 'the Ma who loves babies'. *Ma* was an Efik title of respect and always after, to the end of her days, Mary was known as Ma Slessor or Ma Akamba – the Great Ma.

She saved whatever money she could and adopted the first

of many twin babies, naming her Janie after her sister in Scotland. Her house was like a busy nursery – full of orphans and abandoned children.

One day she was called out to a village about five miles away, where a slave woman named Iye had given birth to twins – a boy and a girl. Mary met the mother as she was being hounded through the forest by a howling mob of men and women. Her property and clothes had been destroyed and she was carrying the babies in a box. Mary took the box and helped the woman along to the Mission House, but they could not take the usual path because the villagers would refuse to use it afterwards. So Mary and the mother had to wait in the heat of the day until another path had been cut. The boy was dead, but the girl, who was called Susie after another of Mary's sisters, grew into a bonny little toddler who was the darling of the household. One dreadful day Susie tipped a pot of boiling water over herself. Nothing could be done to save her and she died of shock and scalding wounds. Mary grieved deeply. She wrote at the time:

My heart aches for my darling. Oh, the empty place and the silence and the vain longing for the sweet voice and the soft caress and the funny ways. Oh, Susie! Susie!

Mary bought Iye, the slave mother, for £10 and freed her, and she remained ever afterwards in the Mission House, a faithful worker and Mary's good friend.

Finally, by dint of her sheer persistence, determination and sense of Divine Purpose, she persuaded the chiefs in the river towns to institute a law against the killing of twins. This was done through the British authorities and with the cooperation of a secret, very powerful society called Egbo, which was notorious and feared for its cruel treatment of women and children. Mary takes up the story in a letter she wrote to her Sunday School children in Dundee:

Just as it became dark one evening I was sitting in my verandah talking to the children, when we heard the beating of drums and the singing of men coming near. This was strange, because we are on a piece of ground which no one in the town has a right to enter. Taking the wee twin boys in my hands I rushed out, and what do you think I saw? A crowd of men standing outside the fence chanting and swaying their bodies. They were proclaiming that all twins and twin-mothers could now live in the town, and that if any one murdered the twins or harmed the mothers he would be hanged by the neck. If you could have heard the twin-mothers who were there, how they laughed and clapped their hands and shouted, 'Sosoşo! Sosoşo!' ('Thank you! Thank you!'). You will not wonder that amidst all the noise I turned aside and wept tears of joy and thankfulness, for it was a glorious day for Calabar.

However, when I gave birth to Simon all those years later, the practice of killing twins had still not been entirely stamped out – witness the plight of Eunice's babies who had slept for one night only in the little room next to mine at Anua Hospital.

Mary's letter continues:

A few days later the treaties were signed, and at the same time a new King was crowned. Twin-mothers were actually sitting with us on a platform in front of all the people. Such a thing had never been known before. What a scene it was! How can I describe it? There were thousands of Africans, each with a voice equal to ten men at

home, and all speaking as loudly as they could. The women were
the worst. I asked a chief to stop the noise. 'Ma,' he said, 'how I fit
stop them women mouth?' The Consul told the King that he must
have quiet during the reading of the treaties, but the King said
helplessly, 'How can I do? They be women – best put them away,'
and many were put away.

And the dresses! As some one said of a hat I trimmed, they were
'overpowering'. The women had crimson silks and satins covered
with ear-rings and brooches and all kinds of finery. The men were
in all sorts of uniform with gold and silver lace and jewelled hats and
caps. Many naked bodies were covered with beadwork, silks,
damask, and even red and green table-cloths trimmed with gold and
silver. Their legs were circled with brass and beadwork, and unseen
bells that tinkled all the time. The hats were immense affairs with
huge feathers of all colours and brooches.

The Egbo men were the most gorgeous. Some had large three-
cornered hats with long plumes hanging down. Some had crowns,
others wore masks of animals with horns, and all were looped round
with ever so many skirts and trailed tails a yard or two long with a
tuft of feathers at the end.

It must have seemed to the slight woman from Scotland a world
away from the life she had led before. Although Mary didn't
really approve of all this over-the-top behaviour and dress, she
admits a grudging admiration:

Such splendour is barbaric, but it is imposing in its own way.
Well, the people have agreed to do away with many of the bad
customs they have that hinder the spread of the Gospel. You must
remember that it is the long and faithful teaching of God's word that
is bringing the people to a state of mind fit for better things.

Before Mary puts out her lamp she writes with simplicity and true humility: *Now I am sleepy. Good-bye. May God make us all worthy of what he has done for us.*

Time passed, and Mary was again invalided home to Dundee after more bouts of fever, but so fearful was she for Janie's safety that, in spite of the new laws she took the little girl home with her. Janie became a regular at the meetings Mary spoke at, passed around from hand to hand as the elegantly dressed ladies in particular oohed and aahed over her black skin and wiry curly hair.

When Mary was fully recovered, she set sail with Janie for Creek Town, Calabar, where she heard the news that her mother and all her siblings had died. There was now no close family left in Scotland for Mary to worry about and send money to, and so she devoted herself entirely to her missionary work. Her simple home became filled with boys and girls whom she had rescued from sickness and death, as well as escaped slaves, abused women, and people looking for cures for their illnesses, many of whom had travelled vast and dangerous distances to be with Ma Akamba.

She went alone to the wild and savage district of Okoyong, noted for its lawless heathenism, having pleaded with the Mission Leaders in Duke Town to be allowed to go. It was during this time that she became known as the White Queen of Okoyong. It is hard to believe that the timid girl who was frightened to go out on Guy Fawkes Day in Dundee because of the crowds parading the streets, could now plunge willingly and fearlessly into the Heart of Darkness. She lived in a mud room, overrun with rats, lizards, beetles, snakes and all sorts of biting insects. She couldn't get away from the squabbling, the bad language and rioting of the wives and slaves in the village and was often tired and ill. There was drinking, debauchery, killing and torture, but she carried on, fortified by the example of her Lord and Saviour, who had come down to earth to save sinners.

Years later, she again returned to Scotland, this time with four little girls, Janie, Mary, Alice and Maggie. She was a famous person now, speaking at packed meetings where hundreds gathered to see and hear the pioneer who had lived alone amongst savages.

'If you are ever inclined to pray for a missionary,' she once told a huge crowd, 'do it at once, wherever you are. Perhaps she may be in great peril. Once I had to deal with a crowd of warlike men in the compound, and I got strength to face them because I felt that someone was praying for me just then.'

Although Mary was now frail, often racked with fever and chills, she served the Lord tirelessly. She helped in the building of the Mission House and Church in Itu, living whilst the building went on in a mud hut with a table, one chair and a few pots and pans. She acquired a bicycle, learned to ride it and pedalled far and wide healing the sick, teaching, praying and converting 'heathens' to her brand of loving and compassionate Christianity.

Because of her reputation and influence among the local people the British Crown appointed her a magistrate, and the former weaver from Dundee became the only woman judge in the British Empire. She was unique, having no books or written precedents to guide her in her work, only her knowledge of the laws and customs of the people and her own Scots good sense.

Ill health once again forced her back to Scotland, but in spite of her fragility she was determined to go 'home' to Africa.

She returned to Use, which became her last home. It was a lonely place set amongst huge grey cotton trees bordering a great highway that ran past a hidden village – hidden because the people still feared slave hunters. Here she carried on as if she were a young, strong girl. One day, a small yellow kitten was brought to her, mewing piteously. It became Ma's faithful friend and companion, always travelling with her, lying in a canvas bag at the bottom of the canoe or draped around her thin shoulders.

She did all the tiresome Court business, sometimes sitting for eight hours at a stretch listening to the evidence; she held palavers with chiefs; she went long journeys on foot into the wilderness, going where no white person had ever been. On Sundays she preached at ten or twelve villages, and in between times she was making and mending, nailing up roofs, sawing boards, cutting bush, making mud walls and laying cement.

One day she received an important-looking official envelope. When she opened it she found that she had been awarded the Silver Cross of the Order of the Hospital of St John of Jerusalem. She travelled down to Calabar to receive the prestigious award, terrified at the prospect of having to take part in a public meeting. But she was delighted to be presented with a bouquet of roses that she took home to Use where she planted a cutting. Although she was now growing deaf and blind, and was constantly tired and weak, she was running three missionary stations, Use, Ikpe and Odoro Ikpe.

These are some of her diary entries at the time:

Left the beach for Ikpe in the evening, sail in moonlight; reached Ikpe 4pm next day; ran on to a tree; boys thrown into the water. Egbo out all night, screaming and drumming like madmen till daylight. All drunk.

First night in new house. Sorry to leave the wee hut I have enjoyed so much comfort and blessing in.

Patients from early morning; man bitten by rat; another by snake.

School begun, nearly a hundred scholars.

First Christian funeral at Ikpe.

Chiefs here by daybreak for palavers.

Splendid congregation. People changing for the better.

Terrific thunderstorm. School-boys drenched. Got a big fire on in hall, and all sat round the blaze and I gave them a reading lesson.

A great reception at Use – thank God for the girls and home. Thank God for sleep!

On roof all day, head and neck aching, hands broken and bleeding. Carrying sand, cleaning corn patch, mudding and rubbing walls.

Cut my first two roses from the rose bush – lovely, a tender gift from God.

After sleepless night found white ants in millions in the drawers.

Washed a big washing.

Terrific rain storm, no school.

Very feeble, scarcely able to stand upright in church.

Horrid night with cross child.

Lovely letters from dear ones. God is very good to me.

Every boy in school clothed to-day for first time.

Heaps of sick babies.

Full up with work till late at night. Dead tired.

Two women murdered on the way from market and their heads taken away.

Fever; trying to make a meat safe.

Sleepless night, baby screaming every few minutes.

Splendid fever-sleep full of dreams. Thank God for daily strength to go on however feeble.

Thank God for the girls who got up and got me tea without any bother.

Reached Rest House at darkening. A fearful night of misery with mosquitoes, and hard filthy ground on which we lay. Rose at first streak of dawn and never was so glad to leave a place. Baby yelled all night.

Nothing done, low fever, but a very happy day.

Fever, stupor sleep. Lost count of days.

Useless after utterly sleepless night. Made such sermons and delivered them all night long.

Her house at Odoro Ikpe was almost finished. It was August 1914, and strange stories of a war in Europe were circulating. Mary now became desperately ill. Her girls decided that she must be taken home to Use. Her camp bed was lifted and placed gently in the canoe that was to take her home. Her beloved yellow cat, the companion of so many of her long hours and desperate nights, ran into the bush and was never seen again. All day her frail form was paddled down the creek among the water lilies, and at night they laid her in the white moonlight on the beach. When she had regained a little of her strength, they carried her the three miles to Use.

She died in Use. Her body was taken down the Cross River to Duke Town, where she was buried on the Mission hill. Her gravestone, carved of grey granite from Scotland, is still there today, a testament to a remarkable heroine.

I was twenty-five years old when I first stood on that hill above the river and gazed at Mary Slessor's grave. I had no idea who she was, where she had come from, or what she had achieved. But, subsequently, I was to teach not only at Duke Town

Secondary School, beside the spot where Mary had first settled, but also at Hope Waddell, the famous teachers' training school for boys which Mary had started when she was living in Calabar.

It was the people of Calabar who told me her story. Her dear friend, Mr MacGregor, gave perhaps the best description: *'She was a whirlwind and an earthquake and a fire and a still small voice, all in one.'*

What drove Mary? Certainly she had dreams, as we all do. Not daydreams that vanish into thin air and are soon forgotten, not dreams of the night that disappear when we wake up, but dreams – perhaps visions would be a better word – that motivated her, inspired her and that she translated into the reality of her life's work. You and I would probably call them ideals. Why did they become reality? Because of her determination and unshakeable belief. But it was not only her belief in God that drove her to achieve the impossible; it was also her unwavering faith in herself.

No matter what your spiritual beliefs, no matter what your circumstances, no matter your particular moment in history, follow your own heart, nurture your own integrity. Nobody, nothing, can take that away from you.

7

'Have A Go!'

Have a Go! was one of Doris' favourite sayings. Whatever opportunity came along, whatever new prospect or untried possibility presented itself, Doris would urge Rita and me to 'Have a Go!' She herself kept on 'Having a Go' until the end of her long life.

At the age of seventy-four (fifteen years before she died) she left England for a year to work as a nanny to the children of an oil sheikh in Saudi Arabia.

'Why are you going?' Rita and I asked her, knowing that she didn't like children very much and that she'd never been a nanny before.

'Because I've never been there,' came the prompt answer. 'And . . .' (the next was pronounced as if it was the most obvious reason in the world) ' . . . I've always wanted to see the desert.'

The first time the Royal Household set out for a picnic in the desert outside Riyadh, Doris was thrilled. The days before the picnic passed in a frenzy of activity. Plans were drawn up, schedules plotted and re-plotted, soothsayers consulted, omens read, and finally the time and place were set. The big day dawned and the royal caravanserai set out with great pomp and in high spirits. My mother's charges, two small male minor scions of the royal family, were washed, perfumed and dressed in flowing white robes and put into one of the many royal limousines and, accompanied by pawing and prancing Arab stallions, the household headed off for the desert – slave girls and all, according to Doris.

When they got there, the silken tents were unfurled and erected, the antique Persian carpets were spread out on the desert sand, the traditional food was laid out, the smoke from the silver burners shimmering in the heat, and picnic baskets, some flown in especially from Harrods, were unpacked. Silver trumpets sounded and the slender silky-haired hunting dogs, the Salukis, were unleashed to run down desert gazelles. The royal falconers stood braced and straight-backed with their fierce, keen-eyed avian charges on their leather-clad wrists scanning the far horizons. My mother watched all this with the wonder for all things new which never left her.

'It was like a film,' she would remember dreamily. 'And then it rained. So we packed everything up and went home.'

I know many people who have changed direction in their lives, either because they'd 'had a go' and found out that they didn't like what they were doing or believing, or because they felt intuitively that they needed a new route, a new way of thinking or behaving.

I was at school with a girl called Bernadette Dickson. (I've changed her name because she is still alive.) She was the only child of a hard-working widow, a woman whose husband had died of lung disease after too many years spent working in a cotton mill in Blackburn in Lancashire. Mrs Dickson had come to live outside St Albans with her only daughter, lured there by the offer of a lucrative job in an aircraft factory.

Bernadette was a clever girl, a devout Catholic and vulnerable to the influence of some of the nuns who taught us. She came under the sway of one nun in particular, the charismatic Mother Annunciata, who taught science at which Bernadette excelled. Mother Annunciata had a thrilling deep voice, cornflower blue eyes and an incisive mind. Bernadette first started talking about becoming a nun as young as ten or eleven, always encouraged by her influential mentor.

By the time she was sixteen, her mind was made up. She would enter the Loreto Order as a novice after her A Levels and devote her life to Christ. Her waking days and nightly dreams were full of her ambition. Nobody said the rosary as devoutly as Bernadette did. Nobody spent longer on her knees in the school chapel, nobody walked so reverently and piously in the Children of Mary Easter procession, nor sang with greater fervour at Midnight Mass.

Mrs Dickson was proud of her daughter on the one hand, apprehensive about her closed future on the other. All her friends gave Bernadette a huge going-away party. We admired her, believed in her, even envied her, and to some extent, were humbled by her devotion and commitment.

Bernadette lasted exactly one year as a novice. I saw her after she 'jumped over the wall', as it was known in those days, but she spoke very little about her experiences except to admit that she 'had made a terrible mistake' and that it had been very hard for her to come to that realisation and then make the decision to leave. She became a student at the London School of Economics, perceived in the Fifties and Sixties as a hotbed of radicalism and communism. She abandoned her religion, became a card-carrying member of the Communist Party, a well-known student activist, and finally ended up happily and successfully as a Labour Member of Parliament. She never married.

I know another nun who abandoned the cloisters because she felt she had chosen the wrong path in life.

Her name is Pam. Pam was raped when she was ten years old, but buried the dreadful experience deep in her subconscious, and finally entered a Carmelite convent when she was nineteen. It was a tough decision to leave her home and secular state in Johannesburg where she was a successful musician and music teacher to join the closed order of Carmelite nuns. Her family and friends were horrified.

'How can you do this? You're not even a Catholic!'

But after much praying, soul-searching and meditation, Pam made up her mind and entered the closed, contemplative Carmelite Order – an order devoted to prayer and silence. She stayed for a little over a year. Her 'best' time was the hour each evening when the nuns were allowed to talk to each other.

'What did you talk about?' I asked her on my radio show.

'About music and literature, philosophy and art. We had some pretty bright women at the convent.'

'Why did you leave?'

'Because I became too anxious.'

'Anxious about what?'

'About the whole religion, about its prescriptive nature. About me. I felt I would never be worthy enough to carry on.'

For the next forty or so years Pam still tried to live a contemplative life, seeking peace and spiritual fulfilment. She found a psychotherapist who allowed her to confront her childhood abuse and to become, as she says, 'a real person again'. During her time at the convent she had never undergone a true spiritual experience. A couple of years ago Pam attended a self-assertiveness workshop. As she sat in one of the lectures, a profound peace and 'kind of ecstasy' transformed her being into one of light, love and spiritual fulfilment.

'It came out of the blue, a true miracle.'

She does not expect to have another such mystical experience, nor is she looking for one.

'Because, for the first time, I now know for certain that God exists.'

Nearly forty years later she talked on live radio about her experiences. Nervous at first, she became more and more confident as she described her subsequent life and her never-faltering relationship with Christ. She wrote to me afterwards:

> *What amazes me is my description of my life's path to the centre of Christ: it flowed so easily and with such understanding, gratitude and joy straight from my heart and head to you and the listeners . . . I really did not know I had arrived at that place – a place I've been working towards for the last 42 years . . .*

Another email arrived a few days later.

> *Dear Kate, after my talk with you, a really nice person called and said her sister, who was a Carmelite, did the unforgivable. She left Carmel and married the Archbishop!*

A few weeks before Pam told us her story, I interviewed Paulo

Coelho, the world-famous Brazilian author, on the line from Paris. His book *The Alchemist* is a tender, gentle story about a shepherd boy who learns to live his dreams. It teaches us how to follow our dreams, to listen to our hearts, to live in the present and to risk what we have to pursue our destiny. Sometimes the young shepherd's search seems foolhardy and doomed to failure, but he keeps his dreams alive until his final meeting with an alchemist in the desert. As a young man Paulo, the author, was confined to a mental institution simply because he was an artist. He was kidnapped and tortured by paramilitaries and had experiences with black magic and drugs.

Had his suffering moulded him in any way? Was he a stronger and better person because of it?

'No,' came his prompt reply. 'Suffering cannot lead us to any place. I have my doubts about suffering as making you stronger and better.'

I asked him about the wavering of faith. Many devoted, believing people lose their faith or feel it becoming shaky at one stage or another. What would his advice be?

'Faith has its ups and downs. You must keep asking, am I connected to my path – whatever that path may be. If I get solid answers I lose the joy of being alive. By being open to life and to people, each day is a miracle.'

When Paulo Coelho's life-enhancing *The Alchemist* was published, it sold a mere one hundred copies in its first year. But Paulo never lost faith in his allegorical fable about a boy seeking truth. He found another publisher, the book struck a universal chord, and has now sold over thirty-five million copies and been translated into fifty-four languages.

'Did you ever lose faith in your book or in yourself?' I ask.

'I sometimes wavered, but I never really lost heart. We're

guided by signs . . . keep looking for them.'

Immediately after we finished speaking and the line to Paris had been cut, a lady called Deirdre called in to the radio station. Yesterday had been the fifth anniversary of her son Gordon's death. Gordon was murdered while trying to save his girlfriend from armed robbers. Deirdre was in tears.

'Yesterday a yellow bird flew into my house and stayed with me for several minutes, completely unafraid. When he finally flew off, for the first time since Gordon's death I've found, I've found . . .' The airwaves were charged with her emotion. But she found the strength to carry on. 'I've found closure of my grief . . .' Another pause. 'And finally acceptance of his death.'

Deirdre, as Paulo Coelho had suggested, had recognised and been guided by her unique signs.

Amyn Dahya believes that he was led to change his life. Born and raised in Kenya, as a boy he sold fresh eggs from the family farm to the tourist hotels along the coastline of Mombasa on his way to school each day. He went on to have a distinguished academic career, graduating with first class honours in chemical engineering at an English university. He formed his own very successful consulting and technology development company and was at the forefront of the scientific commercialisation of strategic water purification technologies worldwide.

But the Wheel of Fortune turned, and Amyn found himself a victim of a harsh takeover, forced to go up against the might of the American legal system. He lost everything and was at the lowest ebb of his life – not only work-wise, but also emotionally, physically and spiritually.

Then something happened to him that changed his life in a very different way. He was again a victim, this time of a potentially fatal motorcycle accident, but as he was thrown up into the air, he felt 'giant hands' catch and hold him gently as he watched his bike in flames below. From that moment on, he felt called to spend the rest of his life as a healer, using his knowledge of water and its power as the basis of his spiritual work. A gentle and humorous man, he now travels the world on healing missions and believes he has cured many people of many different diseases and conditions – from a young Spanish woman diagnosed with terminal cancer, to AIDS sufferers and stroke victims. He believes his inspiration and power come from the 'Origin'.

'I consider myself to be an instrument of the Origin, through whom knowledge, energy and healing is given to those who recognise and seek this special experience.'

Does he believe he is blessed?

'Yes, I have indeed been blessed with many gifts, one of which is to help people heal from their illnesses. My greatest gift is the ability to help people help themselves. Even when I conduct healing sessions, I make it very clear that my role is to help place people in the relay race. They are the ones who are to complete the race!'

Why does he use water as a conduit for his healing?

'Water is the most intelligent element on earth . . . Water has a great number of highly intelligent dimensions, which are linked to the earth's electromagnetic field, the sun, gravity, the intelligence of the environment. Water carries what I call "intelligence fields", which connect us fully to our environment.'

Amyn asks the people who attend his seminars to bring a bottle of natural spring water with them.

'During the healing meditation, the water that each person holds is energised with healing codes that come from water's intelligence field. In this way, when this water is drunk or applied to areas of the body that are unwell, it helps accelerate healing.'

Amyn is just one of thousands of sincere, caring people I have met or interviewed over the years whose lives were changed dramatically. Or who chose to change them. Or who believe that they have changed the lives of others. Not all are as sincere and convincing as Amyn.

I once interviewed a famous American past life regressionist who regaled me with a laundry list of his successes. I think you'll enjoy this particular 'success' as much as I did.

Dr Wayne (not his real name and I believe the academic distinction was self-conferred) practises in Southern California. One day a woman called Betty came to consult him. She had an elephant phobia.

I couldn't help myself.

'Surely to goodness there can't be many elephants in Southern California!'

Dr Wayne quelled me with a piercing look (a look obviously honed and perfected over many years of dealing with sceptics, cynics, non-believers and people with elephant phobias). He patted his carefully sculpted hair.

'I regressed her,' he continued, ignoring my interruption, 'to a past life.'

He related how he had hypnotised and then regressed Betty to this past life. Rewind a million years or so. Betty, it seemed, had been a cave woman. One morning, as she stepped out of her cave, adjusting her skins as the sun came up over the pre-historic horizon, she stopped dead in her tracks, screamed and fainted. A woolly mammoth was charging her. However, Betty's story had a happy ending, because as soon as she realised the source of her primeval phobia, she lost her fear of elephants and continues to live happily in Pasadena knowing that if she does encounter a menacing pachyderm on the way to Walmart, she can handle the situation with ease.

A friend of mine had his life changed in a very unusual and almost inexplicable way.

It is not long after the millennium and I am in Cuba with a small group of friends. Cuba is a magic island, trapped in a Fifties time warp.

The brightly coloured vintage cars – from 1934 Fords to 1950s Chevies – tool along the potholed city roads in top gear. They roar past lumbering Russian trucks crowded with people on their way home from work – it's illegal for a government truck to drive past local hitch-hikers. Ancient horse-drawn carts – an essential part of the island's transport system – clop along with their heavy load of after-work commuters. Oh-so-beautiful girls in skimpy skin-tight clothes – looking as if they're shrink-wrapped – strut their stuff on the broken-down pavements. Macho cowboys with big-brimmed hats and flat bare stomachs trot their thin horses alongside the main arterial highway. There's old-fashioned, blue-dim strobe lighting, very few street lights, a handful of public telephones in the villages and small towns, and the people live in charming traditional little wooden houses with palm leaf thatch or else in ugly little mass-produced concrete boxes. No advertising signs, just huge billboards everywhere proclaiming, reinforcing and glorifying The Revolution.

'Motherland or Death' a towering painted Fidel Castro exclaims, pointing a massive warning finger at passers-by.

'Always The Revolution!' proclaims Cuba's most charismatic hero, the handsome Che Guevara, waving his ubiquitous cigar.

'Comrades Forever!' declare the three heroes of the Revolution, Fidel Castro, Che Guevara and Camilo Cienfuegos, their mighty arms wrapped round each other.

'Lest We Forget' warns yet another colossal sign.

Mountains and tobacco fields, black buzzards with scarlet beaks and scarlet legs continuously wheeling the blue skies, crumbling buildings and newly restored colonial mansions, confident people of every colour and hue – from pale white through honey brown and bronze to dark, dark brown. Old cinemas, shops with nothing to sell, Fifties modernist architecture which is in-your-face plain and bare, often brutally ugly, but the idea is it's designed for the people – it's stuff they can understand. Old Spanish cathedrals and dark doors leading into cool marble hallways. And everywhere – on streets, in houses, on the beach, in hotels, in cafés and bars – the island is alive with the sound of music – Salsa, Afro-Cuban, Buena Vista Social Club, soulful Spanish ballads, cha-cha-cha.

Our Cuban guide Estralita, who went to Russia at the height of the Russian presence in Cuba to study Russian language and literature, only to return five years later to find the Russians had pulled out, tells us some of the fascinating history of the island.

Cuba has a chequered past, moving from Spanish, French and English domination (although the English only held the 700-mile-long island for eleven months), through mega pirate activities (Drake and Raleigh were here along with Captain Kidd) and the Spanish-American War of 1898, to the Glorious Revolution of 1959, which gave Cuba its first ever taste of freedom and communist ideology.

The stories and popular history of The Revolution are legion and perpetuated everywhere. How Fidel, Che and Camilo, with a bare three hundred revolutionaries, captured an armoured train and its load of weapons, fighting off ten thousand of the despot Batista's government troops in the process. How the rebels lived and fought in the mountains, swelling their tiny ranks from hundreds to thousands as the thirst for freedom grew among the people, and how the Revolutionaries went from victory to glorious victory.

The Che Guevara Memorial in Santa Clara in the centre of the island is a living monument to the Argentine doctor who gave his life for the Cuban people and their freedom. (On a mission to Bolivia he was captured by Bolivian soldiers and executed in front of US advisers.) We stand silently at the perpetual flame burning in the cool, quiet, very poignant mausoleum that harbours the ashes of Che and his most famous *compadres*.

After its successful revolution, Cuba aligned itself with Russia, but when the Berlin Wall and Communism fell at the end of the Eighties, the Russians pulled out, leaving Cuba on the brink of economic collapse. Although today it's officially a socialist republic, ironically tourism is its most important industry – a far cry from the days of Russian missile bases and the huge nuclear power station which still dominates the skyline outside the port of Cienfuegos, on Cuba's Caribbean coastline.

Havana itself, once the most important Caribbean outpost of Spain's New World empire (Christopher Columbus landed here in 1492), a transit point for troops and treasure, is a city in violent transition. When we visit Habana Vieja, the historic heart of Cuba's capital city, on the one hand we feel part of

Havana's romantic past; on the other, as if we are in the middle of a gigantic building site. Crumbling old mansions of Spanish grandees and sugar barons (recently five hundred buildings fell down in Havana in one year alone) are now rabbit warrens of small apartments whose once-grand and glorious facades are festooned with washing. Alongside are newly restored buildings of breathtaking elegance and balance.

The task of Eusebio Leal, official historian of the city of Havana, proclaimed a UNESCO World Heritage Site in 1982, is to restore and protect its historical buildings and at the same time to stimulate the life and economy of the different historic areas without destroying their original ambience – a daunting task given the influx of the Yankee dollar and such capitalist chains as Benetton.

In Lenin Park in the centre of the newer city, a life-size bronze statue of John Lennon holding a flower sits quietly on a bench. Inaugurated only a few years ago, the statue is a tribute to the Beatle's silent role in The Revolution – young people saw him at the time as a symbol of youth and freedom. The words of his song 'Imagine' are etched into the pavement at his feet. In the Sixties, I interviewed the Beatles when they were first beginning to be famous. I particularly remember John and Paul, whose intelligence and spirit shone brightly. Full of life and promise, they came into a small BBC recording studio and played live 'She loves me, Yeah, Yeah, Yeah'. There was no miming in those days – everything you saw was live and real.

Now over forty years later, I sit beside this life-size John Lennon, am drawn to put my arm round his cold bronze shoulder and feel tears roll down my cheeks.

Life, if we let it be, is such an amazing journey and takes us to such unthought-of places. Never in my wildest dreams, when as a young woman myself, I first listened to those young men playing, could I have possibly imagined the present moment and my own life journey to it. I look down at my feet and see that powerful word 'Imagine' written in stone.

Trinidad, a little town south-east of Havana, is another UNESCO World Heritage Site. It's a tiny town with uneven cobbled streets leading up to the main square paved with pink Spanish tiles, once used as ballast in the old sailing ships. Surrounding the minuscule square are wrought-iron railings brought from seventeenth-century Philadelphia. The locals raised the money by raffling a gold doubloon. Yellow, honey-coloured, pink, brown and blue buildings surround the square that is dominated by the old Spanish cathedral – the richest church in Cuba because of its twelve hand-carved wooden altars. A woman dressed all in white – a member of the Afro-Cuban Santeria religion – offers me a 'lucky' necklace of seeds and pods to ward off evil spirits.

In the far west, in Pinar del Rio province with its fertile soil and verdant tobacco fields, we visit a cigar factory. Every part of the cigar-making process is done by hand. Six people to a row, cardboard over the window frames, a supervisor in each room to make sure the day's cigar quota is achieved (95 for big cigars, 135 for small ones). A couple of young workers enjoy a long kiss as they roll their respective cigars. In the morning an official Reader reads the news to the workers, in the afternoon it's a novel or poetry. All Cuban, of course.

I've always enjoyed the works of Ernest Hemingway, so it was a particular thrill to visit his house just outside Havana, where the Nobel Prize-winning author lived for more than twenty years and where he wrote *The Old Man and the Sea*. It's a cool Spanish colonial house overlooking the sea, preserved just as he left it in 1960. Thousands of books – well worn and obviously well read – line the white walls and paintings of all kinds (particularly of bullfights), a plate by Picasso, and the heads of his game trophies adorn the walls. Beside his favourite armchair his original rum bottles stand together on a handy trolley – you feel as if he'll be back at any moment. We see his boat, with the ubiquitous bar set next to the wheel, and learn that Gregorio Fuentes, his skipper and lifelong friend, was here just last week. He is now 103. We see the pool where Hollywood legend Ava Gardner swam naked, watched by an appreciative Hemingway and cronies.

In these early years of the twenty-first century Cuba is on the cusp. On the one hand, it's an admirable socialist state with over 95 per cent literacy for all its people, free medical care, free education, subsidised food and housing. OK, you have to queue up with your ration book to get your basic foodstuffs, and your transport (if you can find any) will probably be a very old truck, a hideously overcrowded long bus with a hump in the middle called a 'camel', a horse, a bicycle, a wagon, an old car or your own two feet. But if your belly is full, the sun is shining, the rum is good and cheap and there's music to be made – well, it's a good life in a way. On the other hand, you can't leave the island without permission, and the stuff of intellectual stimulation is rare (few books, only two government TV channels). It's difficult to learn about other places and cultures when you're so cut off from the rest of the world. And there must be some cogent reason why thousands of Cubans have sailed across the sea – often on rickety rafts – and are now living in Miami.

We visit Varadero, the main tourist beach resort 40 kilometres east of Havana. It's beautiful but bland, designed for lower-end-of-the-market European and American package tours whose clients' sole desire is to escape a northern winter, boil themselves lobster-red on the white sandy beaches and then fly back to Luton, Madrid, Kansas, Toronto or Dusseldorf without ever seeing any other part of the island. However, Estralita has told us there might be an opportunity to swim with dolphins off Varadero's coastline and we were determined to try.

And that is where and when Philip's life changed.

Philip was a very successful, late-fiftyish businessman. Although he was good company and often full of fun, I could sense there was a darker side to his nature, one that revealed itself in morose moments, too many cocktails and whispered rows with his young blonde girlfriend.

Early one morning, eight of us take a small boat out to sea for a day excursion. If we are lucky, our cigar-chewing Antonio Banderas lookalike skipper tells us, we might get to swim with dolphins.

The small boat chugs out to sea for a couple of hours over a startlingly blue sea, gulls diving and calling, the sunny day wearing on, until we finally reach a huge, wooden enclosure in the middle of the sea where dolphins have been trained to take fish from the hand but are free to come and go as they wish. Our skipper removes the stub of his cigar and blows a whistle. Suddenly we are surrounded by a school of dolphins. The skipper feeds them fish whilst the other crew member lowers a small ladder over the side.

'You can swim now,' says the captain, reinserting his cigar as he adjusts his frayed straw hat over his eyes, sits down, leans against the side of the boat, shuts his eyes and dozes off.

Only Philip is nervous. A former athlete, still very fit, a

116

three-times-a week squash player, he seems reluctant to go over the side. Finally, after much persuasion, he gingerly climbs down the ladder (most of us have jumped off the side), enters the water and swims a small distance away from the boat. The dolphins immediately target him. Although they have been playing with the rest of us, chattering to us and nosing us, even turning over on their backs for a tummy scratch, as soon as Philip enters the water, they all turn their attention to him. They swim round him, considering him, even judging him, it seems. He treads water nervously. Then they begin to nudge him gently and softly shoulder him. After a few moments of this Philip visibly begins to relax. Then one dolphin lifts her long grey nose out of the water and 'kisses' his cheek. She swims round him, talking her squeaky language to him, bumping him gently, encouraging him and 'kissing' him. The others soon lose interest and come back to play with us, but Philip's dolphin never leaves him, talking to him, circling him, coming back again and again to kiss him. It seems as if she knows Philip has a problem and she wants to comfort him and advise him.

For the rest of the trip, and to this day, Philip is a changed man. He believes that 'his' dolphin told him something that resolved his emotional difficulties. He had a moment of enlightenment. He has never told me what she communicated to him, but it changed his life.

He abandoned his trophy babe and went back to his wife.

The lives of both Amyn and Philip were changed in dramatic ways. Not all of us are lucky enough to be shown a new beginning so clearly.

But I believe that there are always opportunities for change. Look for them, and 'Have A Go!'

8

The Land That Time Forgot

When you were growing up, did you ever wonder what you would do when you were an adult, where you would live, what places you would visit? Because of Doris' influence ('Have a Go!') it never occurred to my sister Rita and me, growing up in rural England, that there were places that some people might baulk at visiting, let alone going to live there. I thought I had some idea about Africa – after all, had I not read *King Solomon's Mines*, *She*, *Heart of Darkness* and *Tarzan of the Apes*? But I had precious little knowledge of Nigeria, let alone New Guinea.

Yet when the time came, Rita and I set off for our exotic destinations as happily as others would set off for the local market. After all, you never know what's around that next corner.

There's a great bird-shaped island lying to the north of Australia. Around it, above and below it, are hundreds of other islands – large and small – but none is so big or mysterious as the great bird-shaped one that is Papua New Guinea.

Just after I had gone to live in Nigeria, in the mid-1950s, my sister Rita found herself in New Guinea, thousands of miles from where I was, but where magic and sorcery were also rife, where strange, ancient rituals were still performed, and tribal disputes fought with bows and arrows, spears and clubs.

The indigenous people she found herself among ranged in colour from coal-black to golden-brown, and in shape from slender and delicate to small and chunky. In some areas, faces and bodies were marked with tribal tattoos in elaborate patterns; in other areas, scars and weals were woven into significant designs all over the body. Noses were decorated with flat discs of bone, or pierced with large, horizontal bones, and ears were stretched and elongated.

Several inland tribes, known as the Kukukukus, were fierce and skilful warriors who went into battle wearing bark cloaks. *Kukukuku* is a Motuan word for the huge cassowary bird, and the warriors wore the thick leg bones of this bird for both glory and armour. They also dried their dead and carried them around with them.

In the steaming swamplands on the eastern tip of the mainland lived the cannibal Orokaiva, who terrorised the surrounding tribes and who wore spectacular headdresses of birds' feathers and beetles, sometimes decorated with whole stuffed birds. The people of Goroka practised a strange ritual of swallowing lengths of cane, while the Telfomin and the Mainmin raided along the Sepik River, measuring their skill in human heads. The Highland women cut off joints of their fingers as a mark of mourning and others in the Highlands ornamented themselves with great wigs made of human hair decorated with flowers, and used Stone Age weapons fashioned with consummate craftsmanship.

For centuries, New Guinea, with its key position at the junction of Asia and Australia, was the crossroads of the Pacific. Thousands of migrating peoples, from Australian Aborigines and the original Tasmanians, to the Polynesians and Melanesians, left their cultural and demographic mark. The majority of these early people stayed on the coast, but some made their way through the swamps and up into the high peaks and plateaus of the mountainous interior. Huge mountains and dangerous rivers formed geographical barriers between these peoples, and some seven hundred mutually unintelligible languages developed.

Groups living only a few miles apart in the Highlands, but separated by deep gorges, knew little of each other. There was no common language, no concept of community grouping beyond the village, no spirit of cooperative enterprise. Religious beliefs were little understood by outsiders and seemed to have little common currency between different tribes.

But the country was beautiful beyond belief. Hundreds of turbulent tropical streams pour down the jagged mountains whose sides and clefts are festooned with moss forests. In this silent, dripping, almost eerie world grow some of the world's rarest orchids and rhododendrons. The New Guinea forests also provide fuel and material for houses and canoes, vines for bridges, the raw material for weapons and clothing, nuts and fruits, and the materials for medicine, magic and adornment. There are volcanoes, hot springs and geysers, tropical rain-forests, and in the lower, drier areas there are brown savannah grasslands and eucalypts where you could almost imagine yourself to be in Australia.

It was to this strange, beautiful country, to a tiny place called

Minj in the Western Highlands of New Guinea, that my newly married sister Rita, then aged twenty-six, and her husband Jock MacGregor came to live.

Rita's life journey had been more complicated than mine. After leaving London University, where she had graduated with a BA honours degree in English literature, followed by a Diploma in Anglican Divinity and a Dip Ed, she had become engaged to an Australian seaman called Spike – as unlikely a match as one could hope to find – and was planning to go to Australia to live.

By this time, with two daughters safely ensconced in universities with adequate financial support from scholarships, and following the sudden death of Dick, Doris had emigrated to Australia.

When Rita had gone down from university she planned to go to Australia to join Doris. Both had been accepted for the £10 immigrant boat fare with which so many Poms went to Australia in the Fifties, lured there by sunshine, open spaces and the promise of work. Rita had met Spike one Saturday night in The George in Wanstead, where we were both working as barmaids, serving pints and 'shorts' and chatting up the regulars. He never knew what hit him, and once Rita had set her sights on him, it was as if he was tied to the tail of a comet.

He went back to Sydney first, but by the time Rita got there, the idea of Spike as a life partner had begun to lose its appeal, and she took herself off to the School of Pacific Administration in Sydney where she met Jock. She was appointed as an Education Officer in the Education Department of Papua New Guinea and Jock landed a job as a Patrol Officer in New Guinea, a territory his late explorer grandfather had traversed exhaustively looking for gold. Gold had been discovered at Wau, Bululo and Edie Creek in 1923, and it gave the spur not only to the development of air transport but also to the hopes of Jock's Scots grandfather. At one time there were eight specially designed dredges working in the Wau–Bululo area, all of which had been flown in, piece by piece in Junkers aircraft, and then reassembled. The gold industry was at its height when Japan entered World War II, but subsequently lost its importance when both New Guinea and Papua became bloody battlefields.

When Australia took over New Guinea in 1946, there were still vast areas that had never been penetrated or explored by Europeans. Australia now saw it as her social and political duty to bring law and order to tribes and tribesmen in the most remote and inaccessible places. Jock, assisted by indigenous staff, slogged on foot through patrols that often lasted several months, establishing contact, setting up patrol posts and bringing Progress to the local people. Many of the houses were communal – the 'long houses'. There were houses for courting, where chaperoned young couples engaged in love-play; spectacular ceremonial structures such as the magnificent *haus tamberan* of the Sepiks; and low squat huts which even the pygmy-like people had to stoop to enter. At the famed Mount Hagen show, where thousands of people from all over the Highlands area congregated to dance, sing and celebrate their indigenous cultures, guest houses were built sometimes half a mile long.

Rita wrote me long letters about her new life, a life in its way even stranger and more intimidating than the one I was living in Itu, surrounded by the strange, outcast Oşo.

In those days, the eastern half of New Guinea, formerly a Crown Colony, was called the 'Territory'. In 1946, the United Nations had approved the terms of a Trusteeship Agreement that made New Guinea a Trust Territory administered by Australia. Port Moresby in the south-west was the capital, located on hills along the eastern and northern shores of a large, almost landlocked harbour. When Rita and Jock first flew to Port Moresby, they presented their credentials to the relevant government department at Konedobu, only a short distance from the local village of Hanuabada, where houses were built on stilts over the sea and numerous houseboats with crab-claw sails dotted the skyline. But it was in the Highlands that Rita and Jock made their home.

Not far from where my sister lived was a narrow airstrip perched on a mountain ridge, and this is how my sister and I kept touch over those strange, separated years – by airmail letters. Flying conditions in the Highlands of New Guinea were hazardous to say the least, because of the high mountains, thick clouds and swirling winds, but our letters somehow arrived and survived.

Rita and Jock lived in a square house with walls made of plaited palm fronds, a thatched roof, slightly raised off the ground on wooden posts so as to discourage the New Guinea wildlife.

Rita was soon pregnant and a few months after I had delivered Simon in a tiny mission hospital in the wilds of Nigeria, my pregnant sister flew to Port Moresby on the coast and also delivered a son. She sat knee to knee on the journey to the coast with a local chief in full headdress, the ubiquitous bone through his nose and a tethered, but squealing pig on his lap.

'That's the way we always travelled,' she told me years afterwards. 'It was the only way . . .'

I treasure a photograph of her taken a few months later wearing a silky dress and pearls and holding her baby William outside her little home in the Highlands, whilst the cook, who also doubled as a nanny, looks on fondly. His expression is that of any child-carer looking on at his tiny charge. His face is warm and kindly, an effect spoilt somewhat by the bone through his nose and his Bird of Paradise headdress. Rita looks as if she belongs in the pages of the latest *Tatler*, except for the towering mountains, the dangling palm fringes, the pools of rainwater, her 'garden' of sweet potatoes and taro, and the bone-through-the-nose bystander.

It was thought then, and may still be true today, that the Territory had the most varied collection of insects in the world – there was a good reason for Rita's house to be on stilts. There were vast, exotic swarms of beetles, wasps, bees, ants, flies, mosquitoes, spiders, mites, scorpions, centipedes, grasshoppers, moths and butterflies. Rita, always a romantic, spent some of her days looking for the magnificent Queen Alexandra Butterfly, believed to be the largest in the world. Its brown wings with yellow spots spread to ten inches, and collectors shot them down with special shotguns. There were also Angler Spiders that catch moths with a blob of glutinous liquid hung on the end of a single thread. And then there were snakes such as the New Guinea Death-adder, and lizards, true dragons, the Komodo Monitors whose skin was much prized for drum heads. Even in those days, the birds of the Territory were legendary, particularly the unbelievably beautiful Birds of Paradise – shy, mimicking birds with magnificent plumage. Their courtship dance is very similar to that of the Bower Bird (which makes a colourful garden for its would-be mate) but the Birds of Paradise perform their mating dances in trees instead of on the ground.

All these natural wonders of the world were hardly known to us then – those were the days before TV's Discovery Channel and National Geographic. Rita once sent me some Bird of

Paradise feathers. I collected the tattered brown paper parcel from the post office in Calabar. Although faded and somewhat dilapidated, those feathers boggled the imagination. Scarlet, honey-coloured tipped with black, golden and green, iridescent black and deep purple – they had travelled over such vast distances to reach me. I tried to preserve them but the white ants triumphed. (Another parcel arrived one day containing a tiny brown shrivelled object like a dry orange. It made me shudder and I put it in a box at the back of my wardrobe. I never dared ask Rita what it was. Luckily, the white ants ate it too.)

Rita wrote to me about the Cargo Cults – a cultural phenomenon much researched and documented today, but little known in the mid twentieth-century. The Cargo Cult based itself on the belief that only the white man had access to and power over the material goods that were transported by aeroplane and ship. These were secrets that were kept from the local people, who believed that the cargo came from some mysterious source, but was then intercepted and used by the white man. Some of the local people built airstrips to receive the planes that would bring the goods to them. Rita wrote that one local chief had killed all his pigs and used up or destroyed all his produce in the belief that he had cracked the secret of the Cargo and for ever afterwards would be provided with food and all the luxuries he needed. She had also heard of a chief of a Cargo Cult who claimed to have an egg out of which he would hatch battalions of warriors to drive out the white men who were keeping the secret of the Cargo from them.

'*Batus I-kam!*' (The aeroplane is coming!) was an occasion of excitement, anticipation and great rejoicing.

At more or less the same time that I was visiting the Long Juju of Arochuku, Rita was learning about the masked *duk duk*, a savage secret society that terrorised all who came within its orbit. Like some of the Masks that I saw dancing in Nigeria, members of a *duk duk* society wore long, voluminous habits of grass, bark and sticks, with fearsome painted wooden masks covering their heads and faces. She wrote that the most important things to the local people were land, pigs and women – in that order.

Rita taught English in a little schoolroom where, as the scantily dressed children bent over their slates and books, their parents and sometimes elders of the tribe, be-feathered and often carrying their traditional weapons, watched their children's progress impassively through the open windows, leaning on the window sills while clutching their blowpipes, spears, clubs, and bows and arrows. They were very proud of their children and saw education as a means to prosperity and progress.

Rita wrote some basic English textbooks for her willing pupils, although she often had to communicate in Pidgin English to make her lesson understood. Pidgin English was the lingua franca of the Territory, used not only among the different tribes but also in many administrative publications, instructions on how to vote in national elections, radio broadcasts and even in a commercial newspaper *Nu Gini Tok Tok*. Many expressions were easy to understand. 'Talk' became *'Tok'* so *'tokim'* meant to tell someone something, *'tok kros'* was to scold, *'tok tru'* was to be honest, and *'wantok'* was a person who spoke the same language. From an indigenous word *'bung'* (a meeting place) came expressions like *'bungim ol samting bilong yu'* – put together all your belongings.

Later Rita became principal of the Kavari girls' technical school, a Pidgin English instructor for the Australian Army, and ran adult literacy classes as well.

Two years later, again flying down to the Port Moresby hospital at the last possible moment to give birth, Rita left William in the care of the cook/nanny (Jock was away on patrol) and had a daughter, Catriona. 'Katie' became a successful lawyer and now lives outside Sydney with her English husband and their three small children.

One day *'Batus I-kam!'* announced a very different cargo. Because, of course, it wasn't long before Doris got in on the act. She flew up from Sydney where she had been working in the canteen at Sydney University, and went to help look after William and Katie and to strike fear into the hearts of the unsuspecting tribesmen. She lectured them on the evils of drink (meths was the tipple of choice) and the advisability of smaller families, and even attempted a mini crusade against cannibalistic practices – the eating of the highly prized 'Long Pig'.

'But,' she told me years later, 'our locals had very discriminating tastes. They only ate the tax collectors.'

One of the chiefs asked Jock for Doris' hand in marriage, offering three pigs as a bride price – a great compliment. Doris was thrilled at the honour, but politely declined. A few months later she went back to Australia and the locals settled back into their pre-Doris mode.

Although it was a hard life, Rita, Jock, William and Katie continued to live happily, if unconventionally, in one of the wildest and most remote places on earth.

But then tragedy struck.

One of their friends, a young doctor who had studied with them in Sydney, came to visit. Jock, stripped to the waist, was working in the garden.

'How long have you had that large mole on your back?' Mike asked Jock.

'All my life, but it's been growing a bit lately,' replied Jock in his laconic manner.

A year later Jock died in the Royal Cancer Hospital in Melbourne. It had taken several long, agonising and anguished months for him to fade from a strong healthy young man in the prime of his life to the crippled shell that Rita visited each night after her long day teaching at a girls' high school. There was no money, no pension, and so she was now the sole breadwinner. Auntie Phyllis arrived from England to help look after the children, taking turns with Doris to sit with Jock during the day. Although he lost his physical self, Jock never lost his spirit, but it was a difficult and dark time for all of them.

And so it was that my sister found herself a widow at the age of thirty-four, with no money and two children to support. Always resourceful, she applied for and was subsequently successful in obtaining a post as headmistress of an Anglican girls' school on New Zealand's North Island.

'I knew my theology qualification would come in useful one day,' she wrote to me triumphantly.

But she'd always been a bit of a missionary at heart. After a career of being headmistress at several Anglican girls' schools in New Zealand, Zimbabwe and Australia (her portrait hangs in the entrance hall of St Hilda's School for Girls in Perth to this day), and when William and Katie were grown up, Rita did what her heart had always urged her to do. She went as a teacher and administrator to Elcho Island in the Gulf of Carpentaria in the Arafura Sea, not very far south of New Guinea, where she had lived all those years before.

A mission station had been established there in 1944, but Rita rarely saw eye-to-eye with the missionaries. Although she was a devout Christian, a Deacon of the Anglican Church and had her Diploma in Anglican Divinity, she wrote to me that she found the missionaries incredibly 'narrow-minded and bigoted', making little or no attempt to understand or appreciate the Aboriginal traditions, cosmology or spiritual beliefs.

Understandably, there was no love lost between Rita and the missionaries, but the Aborigines loved and respected her. She was 'adopted' by the local clan and given a totem animal, a whale, symbol of Mother-Father dreaming, not only because of her imposing size and expansive manner but because the whale is a very sacred animal to the local people – the highest animal in the sea. Giving her the whale totem was symbolic of the love and respect they felt for her.

The great black thunderheads which massed overhead before the coming of the rainy season were symbolic of the great black whales which dive and play in the ocean beneath, and represent the great whale ancestor. It was this ancestor who created the clouds by spraying them with the mist from his blowhole, so revealing an intricate pattern of triangles that are still used in ceremonies today. Whale Dreaming sites are found all over Arnhem Land; Rita once took me to one on a reef at Southport, just outside Darwin.

Whales have played a role in my life too. Or, rather, a *particular* whale played a role in my life.

It's a bit of a digression, I know, but I'd really like to tell you about it. You see, I once worked on a whale. Yes, on a whale.

And more than forty years later I was on a ship bound for Antarctica and as we were crossing the notoriously rough Drake Passage on our way to the Antarctic Peninsula, I attended a lecture given by one of the expert guest lecturers on board. The lecture was on whales. He told us, as the ship pitched and rolled, and sleety rain slanted against the windows of the ship's saloon, some of the history of whales and of whaling, and of humankind's preoccupation and ongoing fascination with the great beasts. Earlier that morning, a couple of killer whales – Orcas – had been breaching and blowing around our ship.

'Would you believe,' our whale expert asked the audience, 'that in the Fifties, a dead whale was put on display on the Thames Embankment in London and people paid money to go and visit it?'

The audience gasped in disbelief. People chaffed and tittered. Some of the Jocks from Australia and New Zealand who drove the zodiac landing craft for our shore excursions nudged one another and hooted with laughter. What quaint, amazing things people did in those days!

I put my hand up.

'I worked on that whale!' I told them.

I'd got the job through an advert on one of the notice boards in the Students' Union. It was Easter 1954. Two enterprising young Scandinavians – entrepreneurs supreme when the word had hardly been invented – had found a huge dead Blue Whale – the biggest whale in the world – washed up on a beach somewhere in Scandinavia. I forget exactly where. They had gutted it, put a refrigeration unit inside it and had been carting it around Scandinavia showing it off to the public. It was now doing the rounds of Europe and lay – all 60 feet of it – a bit high and smelly, on London's South Bank.

Our job was to take the entrance fee (half a crown a head) and then to take turns in showing the public around the whale. But the four students who 'worked' on it had been chosen more for their histrionic skills than their knowledge of marine biology.

It was a very hot Easter and we took a sadistic delight in moving our crowds – for crowds there indeed were – from one end of the beast to the other.

'Now, if you'll all move back to the tail . . .'

We were encouraged to tell our own stories of how the Leviathan had met its end. I concocted a story about a pair of aquatic lovers, who mated and then bonded for life, only to run foul of a huge Atlantic storm. The female, Hedda (one of the few female Scandinavian names I knew, courtesy of Ibsen), had fallen foul of the storm and been washed up on a beach where she died keening into the wind for her lost mate.

'To this very day,' I would soulfully tell my flock, 'her mate Lars swims backwards and forwards, backwards and forwards, cleaving the cold, churning waves, his haunted eyes never leaving the lonely beach where his Loved One left him for ever.'

Cheesy, I know, but it went down well in the Fifties when television in England was still young and natural history programmes were few and far between. It's a good thing that in those days we didn't know about the songs of whales. I might have reached even greater Thespian heights – or depths.

After the ticket booths were shut up at night, the four of us used to congregate in Hedda's jaws for a quick beer and a review of the day's proceedings. It was much cooler here than outside. The mighty jaws were fixed open with steel rods in an eternal grimace and as the refrigeration unit hummed in her huge belly on the other side of the curtain of whale bone which hung from the roof of her mouth at the back of her jaws, we joked and laughed away an hour or so.

At the time, we didn't think anything of it. But, looking

back, there can't be many people who have been inside the jaws of a whale and survived. One sunny morning we stood on her back and watched the finish of the Oxford/Cambridge Boat Race. Malcolm, who rowed for his college at Oxford, but didn't quite make it to a Blue, stood with me as we cheered Oxford on. And don't even ask. Of course we had a whale of a time.

What a far cry from Rita's totem animal.

After four years Rita returned to Australia, to Darwin in the Northern Territory where she took up the post of principal of a large new primary school. Her pioneering work in the field of primary education made national headlines when, in the early 1990s, she introduced girls-only and boys-only classes in her school on an experimental basis, to great controversy but with great success.

While Rita had been living and working on Elcho Island, she and her children had been made part of the tribe and given an Aboriginal guardian, whom I will call Alfred, as a living elder may not be called by his tribal name.

After Rita settled in Darwin, Alfred visited the family on only three occasions, each time during a family crisis.

The first visit was just a couple of weeks before I arrived in Australia's 'Red Heart' of Alice Springs to visit my nephew William and his wife Margo. William was a full-on alcoholic, and Margo, who had just found out she was pregnant with her first child, was sick with worry over Will's condition and their personal relationship. One night, there was a tap at the door. Margo opened it to find Alfred standing there. You can imagine her surprise. Alfred had somehow found his way from Elcho Island, and travelled over deserts and swamps to track down William, his 'family', in Alice Springs.

'Leave him,' Alfred told Margo. 'Leave him. Later things will come right.'

And he disappeared into the night.

So leave him she did, going back to her own family down south.

A few weeks later I arrived in Alice Springs to visit Will, who told me the story. Margo had left and he was bitter and distraught.

Six months later, Will was lying in a hospital ward in Adelaide, 'dying' from cirrhosis of the liver. One night, Alfred appeared, seemingly from nowhere, and sat down by William's bed. He stayed with him day and night for a week until it appeared certain that Will would not die. Alfred then vanished as inexplicably as he had done in Alice Springs a few months before.

If you were to drop a plumb line from Elcho Island in the Gulf of Carpentaria, straight through Alice Springs, it would continue to drop straight down to Adelaide – from the very top of the vast continent of Australia to the very bottom. This is the distance that Alfred covered in his custodianship of the MacGregors, distances almost immeasurable and, to this day, none of the family knows where he got his information about their whereabouts.

The last occasion he appeared to the family was in Darwin, just over a year later. It was late October, during *Gunumeleng*, the pre-monsoon season of hot, humid, almost unbearable weather – the 'suicide season'. Rita was sitting alone in her small, air-conditioned house working on a tapestry (which now hangs in my house in Johannesburg). She heard a soft tap on the screen door. She opened it to find Alfred standing there. She thought he was visiting her as part of his custodial duty to the MacGregor family. But no, Alfred had brought Rita a message.

She was to 'go home' that Christmas.

'But I am home,' replied Rita.

'You are to go home to your mother across the sea.'

Rita phoned me as soon as Alfred had left. She was planning to visit us in South Africa for Christmas, a reunion eagerly awaited by all of us. But she told me of Alfred's visit and his solemn message. You can imagine what we thought. Doris, now well into her eighties, lived alone in a little flat outside Brighton in England. Both Rita and I were convinced that Doris was going to die. That was the reason for Alfred's message.

So Rita went back to England just before Christmas. She and Doris had a wonderful week shopping, gazing at Selfridges' Christmas decorations and the other twinkling Christmas lights of London's West End. They went to a matinée performance of *Phantom of the Opera*, and bought themselves a Christmas hamper of goodies from Harrods.

On Christmas Eve, after downing a bottle of Veuve Cliquot (Doris always had style) and a selection of sumptuous goodies from the Christmas hamper, they kissed each other goodnight and went to bed.

An hour later, my sister sat up in bed, called out to my mother, suffered a massive heart attack, and died in Doris' arms.

As Alfred had predicted, Rita had 'gone home'.

After one last wild drinking bout, William became sober. Today, admired, respected, and honoured for his work with street children and Aboriginal law-breakers, he still lives in Alice Springs with Margo and his two children, Jock and Angus.

Rita would have been so proud.

And Doris would have said, 'There you are. Have a Go! You never know what's round the next corner!'

9

A Dolphin, a Bear, a Coyote and a Messenger

When I think about travelling companions, I usually think people. But fellow travellers can also be our thoughts and dreams, our past or present experiences. Sometimes the most powerful fellow traveller is an idea we have, a resolution we've made, or a book or a saying that has resonated deeply and irrevocably with us – I've found out that fellow travellers come in many forms and shapes. Some of them come with us physically, others come with us in spirit or thought. Some will be a great help and solace, others may hinder and distract us from our chosen destinations. Others we may – and sometimes should – discard along the way. A journey is a fluid thing, ebbing and flowing with circumstance and time and so, too, our companions come and go.

I've travelled with hundreds of different people over the years, but each, in some way or another, taught me something about myself, about them, about human nature and the world in general. I've travelled with crazy people, fun people, neurotic people, deeply troubled people, happy people, sad people, shallow people, deep people, disturbed people, and sometimes, not often, with deeply contented people.

My fellow travellers have come from all walks of life – priests, gurus, monks, academics, philosophers, circus clowns, musicians, artists, ornithologists, zoologists, celebrities, celebrity wannabes, taxi drivers, plumbers, ballet dancers, teachers, bankers, butchers and, once, a private detective.

I've travelled with husbands, wives, partners, parents, children – the young and the old. Some of my companions were deeply spiritual people, others less so. Some were deeply spiritual almost without realising it, and certainly not the in-your-face so-called spiritual types who like to declaim their spirituality to the rooftops.

I've travelled with some of the finest people I've ever met, and some of the worst. Some of my fellow travellers were wonderfully memorable – an elderly nun going back to Ireland from Nigeria for the first time in forty years who sat beside me on a flight from Lagos to London; a widower with a terminal illness determined to see the world before he died; a little Vietnamese boy on his way to Holland to his new adoptive Dutch parents; a thirty-something yuppie who had just divorced his wife and had come out of the closet for the first time; a young woman fleeing from her abusive husband.

Some of my fellow travellers were equally memorable because they were Travellers from Hell.

After my first trip to Peru, and the life-changing experiences I met with there (which I relate in *There's More To Life Than Surface*), I was determined to go back. In a way, it was a foolish decision, because you can't go back. As Scott Fitzgerald's Great Gatsby found out, you cannot recreate the past. On the other hand, I learned new things, had new experiences, made new friends and found out more about myself.

This time, however, I went to Bolivia first, before flying on to Peru. As on our previous trip to Peru, we were again a small group – fourteen of us.

It had been a very long flight from South Africa to São Paulo, and after seemingly unending hours of flying, we were in transit in a small airport halfway between Brazil and Bolivia. Our group was standing in a circle, chatting, passing the time, when suddenly a figure in a long purple cloak materialised in the middle of the group like gentian violet ectoplasm.

'Mama!' she screamed, and flung her arms around me. Tears streamed down her dark face as she clung to me with a vice-like grip.

'May I travel with you? I am all alone!'

This was Vera, a thin little Indian lady of indeterminate age from Durban, travelling on the selfsame journey, and unbeknownst to our little group, one of South Africa's best-known hysterics.

And travel with us she did, from the high, windy bleak plains of Bolivia's *altiplano* to Lake Titicaca and its sacred Isla Del Sol, on whose rocky shores were born both Manco Kapac and Mama Ocllo who together founded the Inca Empire, and from the Witches' Market in La Paz to a sacred ceremony in the Peruvian Amazon. No leech could have stuck more firmly to its host or attached itself more deeply than did Vera to us. She finally (and thankfully) vanished as mysteriously as she had come, disappearing like a purple wraith into the crowds at Johannesburg International Airport at the end of our South American odyssey.

The thin air hits you as you walk across the airport tarmac at La Paz Airport – at 14 000 feet, reputedly the highest airport in the world. Dark mountains loom up in the starlit distance as our rickety little bus snakes down the narrow circuitous mountain road towards the town.

'This is our highway,' says Renan, our guide, with no trace of irony.

The driver stops to let us look down from high over the town. It's an evocative and magical sight. In the darkness, thousands of lights twinkle and glow – like Christmas tree lights. There are no huge modern floodlit structures, no brightly lit buildings, just a blanket of tiny twinkling coloured lights like a glow-worm convention. You could imagine thousands upon thousands of hobbits dwelling in those dark hills.

The next morning, still catching our breath in the steep altitude, we explore 'La Cuidad de Nuestra Señora de la Paz' – the City of Our Lady of Peace – which nestles deeply and densely in the Chuquiago Marka Valley, enclosed by a wall of towering, snow-capped mountains.

La Paz is a bustling city of one and a quarter million people, 60 per cent of whom are indigenous 'Indians' – the Aymara; 30 per cent 'mestizo', mixed blood; and ten per cent 'white' (yes, they are called 'whites') of pure Spanish stock.

The main street leading to the Iglesia de San Francisco, the huge church built in 1549, is crowded with people of all kinds. There are elegantly dressed businessmen, street vendors, stall holders at their little kerbside stalls, fashionable shoppers, flower-sellers, tourists, pedestrians of all kinds, including scores of short, stocky Aymara ladies in black bowler hats and huge padded calf-length skirts who look like perambulating hand-bells. It's how you wear your bowler hat that makes the difference. The 'cholitas', the unmarried peasant girls, wear their round brimmed hats jauntily tilted to one side, declaring to the world their unmarried status. The 'cholas' are the staid married women, hats plonked squarely amidships of thick, black, braided hair. Pigtails of young and old alike extend well beyond waist length. Their skirts are thick, thick, thick, of sparkling, brightly coloured cloth – how they get laundered or if they get laundered at all is anybody's guess.

These Aymara faces are small, high-cheekboned, vaguely Asiatic. There is no soft roundness – after all this is a harsh and unforgiving country – except in a few of the children. The faces have flat, sharp, copper-coloured planes and are centred by a small aquiline or hooked nose. It's almost impossible to get anybody to smile, even the children. Life is a serious and hard business in La Paz.

Outside San Francisco, whose huge dome is visible from the highest points in the town, on the cobbled open plaza in the shade provided by its towering facade, 'Fútbol' fans are celebrating noisily. The national team has just won a match against the Peruvian team. Renan remarks pragmatically that Bolivia only won because the classic South American pastime was played at such high altitude that the visiting side was constantly out of breath. As we are constantly catching our own breath, we sympathise with the oxygen-starved losers.

Inside the cathedral fresh flowers adorn every nook and cranny, and kneeling worshippers line the pews. We sit in the cool, sacred silence, away from the ruckus and rumpus outside. As Vera begins to wind herself up into an emotional fit (she has been managing at least one a day), Jo, one of our group, leads her swiftly outside, where her self-induced outburst will be lost in the seething mass of high volume soccer fans. Jo, who speaks

Spanish, skilfully inserts Vera into the cheering throng, passing her off as a particularly ardent supporter, and rejoins us in the cool, quiet interior.

Then on to the Museo De Coca, dedicated to the plant that provides the livelihood for so many Bolivians. The coca plant offers life or death – depending on what you do with it. I first drank coca leaf tea in Cusco in Peru, to help alleviate altitude sickness, and then chewed its bitter-tasting leaves mixed with a paste made from the banana flower when walking in the Andes. But the coca leaf has a far greater power for the people of the Andes than just warding off fatigue, hunger or altitude sickness. The leaves have great symbolic power because they connect humankind to the sacred and divine energies of Andean cosmology, and act as a channel of communication between humans and gods. Excavated burial sites show that coca leaves were used ceremonially thousands of years ago, and today people all over the Andes still use the leaves in their daily lives as well as for ceremony and ritual. This 'wonder' plant with its fourteen alkaloids, all with healing properties, has been grown, harvested and used since time immemorial. Only today has modern man taken, processed and marketed just one of those fourteen alkaloids – cocaine – and in so doing has debased and abused what is still considered a sacred plant by many. The museum is a thought-provoking experience.

Then it's on to the Witches Market – the Mercado de Brujos – just behind San Francisco. Little, twisting lanes are crammed with tiny shops and pavement stalls with Aymara women selling everything from alpaca sweaters, coca tea and reed pipes to handmade bags and silver and gold trinkets. But it's the spells we've come for. We've heard of this one spell in particular. It's called 'The Spell that Destroys Everything'.

'Sounds just the thing for a Bad Hair Day,' says Jo laconically.

'Sorry, Señora, sold out,' the witch tells me. 'Very popular. More next week.'

She points to a puppy-sized shrivelled thing floating about in a glass jar.

'The foetus of a llama. It will cure everything and keep away the bad luck.'

'No thanks.'

She then offers me some crinkly dried llama foetuses but I opt instead for some tiny sealed vials of colourless fluid crammed with all kinds of brightly coloured tiny objects – an amber worm, an orange bean, a red seedpod, a yellow coil, a tiny blue bone, an even tinier golden key. All these objects swirl around and in so doing attract good fortune from the cosmos.

'What happens if I break the seal?' my eleven-year-old grandson Matthew, a great Harry Potter fan, asked me when I gave him one of these spells on my return to South Africa.

'Haven't a clue,' I replied honestly. 'But I wouldn't try it if I were you.'

Three years later the spell still sits intact on his bookshelf.

The next day we rattle along in our rickety little bus – the same one that met us at the airport – over the barren *altiplano* for 75 kilometres until we arrive at one of South America's most fascinating and evocative places – the ruins of Tiwanaku, the former capital of the Tiwanaku Empire that stretched through Bolivia, Peru, Chile and Argentina. It was an astoundingly huge empire with a long history, beginning over 1500 years before Christ, and ending mysteriously just after AD 1100. It was believed to be a warrior state, with a successful agricultural system that fed over eight million people – almost the same number as Bolivia's entire population today.

As we walk through the grey and sandstone-coloured ruins we see imposing courtyards, broken stone pillars, walls of cleverly placed geometric stones similar to those at Sacsayhuaman outside Cusco, the remains of a mighty temple that once stood 18 metres high, where protruding stone heads peer at us from the walls. Three large stone statues cast long shadows on the scorched earth, and Renan tells us that they were probably used to measure time. In the Palace of the Sarcophagi, we marvel at the hundreds of religious designs that decorate its polished stone floor. The monolithic 'Gateway to the Sun', with strange carved inscriptions over its stone rectangular doorway, stands like some inchoate messenger from the past.

Vera, who has been biding her time, now quietly sobs herself into a trance-like state and declares she was once a priestess here. She lies down and stretches out full-length with her arms crossed in a Tutankhamun-like death pose under the vault of the blue sky facing the Sun Gate. A wheeling buzzard eyes her from on high, but nobody else takes any notice.

Massive stones, some weighing up to 130 tons, litter the site. Nobody has yet discovered where these stones came from or how they were moved. All around these lonely relics of a once great and powerful empire the high, dry, windswept plains stretch into the distance as small white clouds scud through a sky of cerulean blue. The buzzard pushes off – he has lost interest.

The altitude is beginning to take its toll. In spite of copious cups of coca tea we all fall into bed that night in readiness for a very early start, because the next morning we are off to the little lakeside town of Copacabana (which shares the same name as the glitzy, rather sleazy beach in Rio) on the legendary Lake Titicaca, the highest navigable lake in the world, 284 metres deep and huge – some eight and a half thousand square kilometres of it.

Titicaca is where the Quechua Indian language and people merge with the more southerly Aymara. After leaving La Paz, we climb first to El Alto, the newest and possibly highest city in the world. A sprawling, ugly, urban eyesore, it's situated on flat high plains which stretch interminably into the distance, dotted by small brown thatched houses, sheep, llamas and dogs. We cross a strait on a small boat crowded with bowler-hatted, crinoline-skirted ladies, and at the other side, there's a small Bolivian oompah band playing. It's some kind of festival. But then, festivals seem to happen all the time in Bolivia. We enthusiastically join in the dancing, but not for long. The barrel-chested, bow-legged locals are built for this altitude, a bunch of African tourists definitely not. We sit down gasping on the cobbles before re-boarding our bus, which has come over the strait on an ancient wooden ferry.

The ride to Copacabana is rough. The bus chugs its way up to 14 000 feet, as we hurtle round hairpin bends, lunge alarmingly towards cliff faces, graze the edges of steep drops and narrowly avoid the oncoming kamikaze traffic. The lake is incredibly blue, sometimes turquoise, sometimes indigo, sometimes violet, sometimes almost purple. I suffer from both altitude and motion sickness, and that night as I lie in bed in our beautiful little hotel of Spanish colonial design, I wish I were almost anywhere else.

'I think I'm dying,' I inform Alan gravely.

'Well, you couldn't have picked a more beautiful spot,' he

reassures me.

The nearly full moon shines on the lake in front of our big windows. It is a scene of surpassing beauty. Everywhere is perfectly still and silent, except for the occasional moonlit ripple on the surface of the lake and a whisper of wind through the fronds of the palm trees. I catch my breath from a chest that feels again, as in Tibet, as if a pair of giant hands is squeezing it.

Dian, recently divorced and grieving, finds her way that night to Copacabana cathedral, where she sits quietly and prays. She feels a palpable healing presence all around her and is calmed and comforted by that presence. Only later do we find out the story of the cathedral. In the sixteenth century, Franciscan missionaries forced the local people to convert to Catholicism. One of the locals, Francisco Yupanqui, carved a statue of the Virgin Mary with Baby Jesus in her arms. But the ethnocentric Franciscans decided that Mary and Jesus looked too Aymara, and ordered Francisco to destroy his statue. Instead, he covered it with a layer of gold and decorated it with elaborate religious images. The Franciscans were fooled and built a church in which to house it. Over the centuries legends sprang up about the statue's healing powers, and today she is kept shrouded in a little chapel at the back of the cathedral and only brought out for her festival in February. Dian did not know about Yupanqui's 'Dark Virgin of the Lake' when she sat alone in the shadowy pew our first night in Copacabana. She just knew that she had found a kind of closure and peace.

Let me tell you about Ryan, another of our fellow travellers. Ryan was in his early twenties at the time of our journey, a startlingly attractive boy with thick dark curly hair and wide green slightly unfocused eyes. His mother, who had saved long and hard for Ryan's journey, had phoned me from Cape Town to ask if it was all right for Ryan to come.

'Why on earth not?' I replied, not understanding.

'Ryan is blind,' she said gently.

She told me that Ryan was a psychic and healer with a well-known practice in Cape Town. I contacted all the other would-be travellers and told them about Ryan. Everybody welcomed his inclusion in the group. Mary, Dian's sister-in-law, a highly energetic, small bundle of Portuguese dynamite, recently widowed, summed up our unanimous reaction.

'It will be an enriching experience for all of us.'

When I wake up next morning on the shores of Lake Titicaca, I feel much better. Renan produces some local *muti* for altitude sickness and I swallow the little green pills thankfully. (I've since observed on my many and varied travels that the local remedy for whatever ails you, always seems to come in the form of little green pills. Maybe somewhere in the Catskills or in an icy cave in Greenland or a grass hut in Cambodia little leprechaun-type creatures are churning out these little green pills in a little factory, thence to be exported to Bolivia, Tibet, India or Vietnam or wherever tourists and travellers get sick. I was once given some identical green pills to those I've just swallowed when crossing the Drake Passage on the way to Antarctica, and more by a Thai boatman when meandering up a river from Chiang Mai to Chang Rai in an old wooden engine-powered canoe.)

We're off to the Island of the Sun, Isla Del Sol, regarded by many as one of the most sacred places in South America, even the world. There are more than seventy islands in the lake, but the Island of the Sun, an ancient Inca temple site, is the largest and most sacred. Our destination is Willa Cocha – Puma Rock. We chug slowly over the sparkling blue water, drinking in the clear air and leaning back against the side of the small boat to face the warm rays of the sun. On the far, far side of the lake, which seems as big as the sea, we pass the much smaller 'feminine' Island of the Moon, framed by towering snow-capped peaks. We anchor in a small bay on the north of the Island of the Sun and then walk for an hour or so southwards along a cliff path that could easily be along the shores of the Greek or Turkish Mediterranean. Steep cliffs rise up from an azure sea, small wooden fishing boats bob in tiny bays and inlets, and gnarled old trees, shaped and sculpted by the prevailing winds, lean against the rocky slopes. Renan tells us that many visitors call Isla Del Sol 'paradise'. It's easy to see why. Apart from the startling beauty of the place there is an all-pervasive atmosphere of peace and tranquillity.

Willa Cocha indeed looks like a huge crouching puma. At the start of our walk we have each been given a small bunch of flowers. These we will now use in the ceremony. Although the sun is hot, a cool little breeze sighs and echoes among the big brown rocks. We sit in a circle in front of Puma Rock on a sandy space high up and overlooking the water. Lake Titicaca spreads endlessly in front of us.

Silently and suddenly, an ancient shaman with a weathered wrinkled face topped by a multicoloured hand-woven cap with ear flaps framing high cheekbones and a beaky nose, appears from the back of the rock. He has a string of large coloured beads round his neck and an embroidered bag with dangling pompoms full of coca leaves and other shamanic substances slung over the shoulder of his pinstriped jacket. He is wearing purple tracksuit pants and cracked brown leather shoes. In one hand he carries a small brass bell, in the other a crucifix. He crouches down, his back to the rock and the lake, and faces our small circle. He looks at us searchingly. Then he carefully unwraps a piece of blue plastic and spreads it out on the brown earth in front of him. He begins to sing and pray, a gentle keening sound that lifts on the wind, whispers past our heads, and floats away into the bushes and trees.

One by one, each in turn, we are beckoned to approach him. Jo is the first. The shaman accepts her flowers gravely, blesses them, raises them up into the air and then places them on the plastic in front of him. He prays for her, murmuring to her. He does the same for each of us as we sit, crouch or kneel in front of him. And then it is my turn. I hear the word 'Pachamama' recurring. The shaman looks at me so closely and deeply that I feel he is looking straight into my soul. Renan acts as interpreter.

'You are a strong woman. You have the power to change other people's lives. Always use that power wisely. But look after yourself. Take care not only of other people but also of yourself.'

He gives me a small brown paper packet containing more little green pills.

When Ryan is led up to the shaman and positioned in front of him, the shaman is silent and still for a long time. At last he places his hands on Ryan's head, traces the planes of Ryan's face with careful fingers, then takes both of Ryan's hands in his own gnarled and knotted ones.

'You are blessed by God. You can heal others.'

None of us had ever set eyes on the shaman before this ceremony, yet he told each of us something deep and true. He comforted Dian, 'It's over. It's over.'

To Alan, my husband, who had nearly died of cerebral

malaria two years before: 'Your sickness is past, but will always be with you.'

At the end of the ceremony, which has been a very moving experience, we hug one another tightly. Then the offering of flowers is neatly folded up, buried in a freshly dug hole and covered with a small rock. We climb down a very steep incline to our boat that has sailed south to meet us, scrambling down over the rocky ground to the lake.

Our boat hugs the coast until we stop at a flight of mud and stone steps cut into the almost vertical hillside. At the top, panting with the effort, gasping in the thin, pure air, we find a tiny inn with wooden trestle tables covered with brightly coloured woven cloths. There are upright logs to sit on. We tuck into homemade soup, *pejerey* ('king' fish) from the lake, and cold beer. After lunch we walk along the cliff top to Templo del Sol, the Temple of the Sun, where once upon a time worshippers gathered from all over the island. The Inca High Priests stood or sat in niches carved into the rock face and gazed out over the immense lake, beyond the high snow-capped mountains, towards infinity beyond. A small boy with obsidian eyes and a snotty nose offers me a 'sacred stone' for two small coins. I take it. It is on my desk as I write.

That night back at our hotel we drink Pisco Sours, a concoction of egg white, lime juice and the local aquavit. Jo's digital camera records a perfect geometric triangle as she photographs the sun setting over the lake. Renan is not surprised.

'We consider triangles to be very sacred and symbolic,' he tells us solemnly. 'It is fitting that you record such a golden triangle over our lake.' And then adds, 'But it has never happened before.'

Cusco in Peru, the 'navel of the universe', has to be one of the most beautiful small cities in the world. The overwhelming visual sensation is of brown – brown-tiled roofs, brown adobe houses, brown cobbled streets and brown mountains encircling and protecting the quaint little town which nestles in a small valley like a brown hen in its nest. Spanish colonial buildings rub shoulders with Inca walls built of mighty, hand-hewn stone boulders; the imposing town square dominated by the squat cathedral leads off into narrow lanes and twisting streets, and pipe music and the cries of vendors fill the air.

There is a fairytale quality to Cusco that reminds me of those line drawings in an old storybook where pedlars sell their wares and children with long hair wander hand in hand. It's difficult to imagine the scenes of carnage, terror and bloody battle that it witnessed when the Spaniards – the Conquistadors – armour-heavy on top of their high horses, led by the ruthless adventurer and explorer Francisco Pizarro, systematically cut down the Inca foot warriors.

Cusco is built in the shape of a puma – one of the great power animals in Inca cosmology – and was not only the capital of the mighty, far-stretching Inca Empire, but also its holy city, a place of pilgrimage. Every ranking citizen of the empire, from Ecuador in the north to southern Chile, and from the Amazon jungles in the east to the Pacific Ocean in the west, aspired to visit Cusco at least once in his lifetime, just as today a Muslim will undertake the Haj pilgrimage to Mecca.

At the Inca ruins of Tampumachay, where sacred springs flow down from the high Andes, and where today empty niches in the walls show where golden statues of their deities once cast fear and awe in the conquered Quechua people, we meet up with six Americans who are joining our party. We sit in a circle at the base of some rocks a short distance from the springs themselves and Carol, the leader of our group, asks us all to introduce ourselves. I seem to be sitting in the middle of a llama midden surrounded by hard little balls of llama dung. It's not very spiritual. From the top of a nearby hill a llama sneers down at me.

'You may use your real name or your chosen one.'

'My name is Dolphin,' announces Gail surprisingly, although I have noticed that ever since we left Johannesburg she has been festooned with dolphin necklaces, bracelets and earrings.

'I'm Big Bear,' announces her husband Paul, who indeed looks like a big, grizzly bear. They've both obviously thought this through and come prepared.

And so we go round the circle.

'I'm Coyote,' announces my husband, turning and grinning at me.

We silently remember a trip to a Native American Medicine Wheel in Sedona, Arizona, where Deborah, our half-Cherokee guide, told Alan that he certainly belonged to Coyote Medicine. In Native American lore Coyotes can be deceptive. They have a facade of intelligence and honesty, but really are full of fun and tricky. My daughter Tiffany and I had hooted with laughter at the time, seeing Alan's crestfallen face. He cheered up, however, when Deborah went on to say that Coyote, sometimes called the Trickster and the Sacred Fool, was also playful, curious and loved to test boundaries. And that Coyote Medicine also represents lateral thinking, creativity and flexibility.

Now it was my turn.

'I'm Kate, I said simply, wondering wildly if I should have given myself some more mystical or spiritual name.

I see a couple of the Woo-Woo Americans immediately labelling me 'boring'.

Bubbly Jeanine and her quiet thoughtful childhood friend Jan, both from Johannesburg, also give their own names.

But Vera, of course, had a field day.

She stood up, still in the ubiquitous purple cloak (rather grubby now) and declaimed in a deep, throaty voice, 'I am Vidya. I am the knowledge by which you on your path can discern the true from the false. I have so developed my spiritual and mental faculties that I can show you the way. I . . .'

I switched off and eyeballed the llama on high.

Vera/Vidya took the grassy floor for a few more moments until Carol politely asked her to desist.

She sat down, wrapped her cloak around her in an extravagant gesture, and gazed meaningfully into the middle distance. The llama made a strange sound between a whinny and a cough. I swear it was a value judgement.

The African-American sitting beside me was 'Messenger'.

'Why Messenger?' I asked him later.

'Because I'm a Messenger of the Gods.'

Take that. End of conversation.

For a couple of years after our trip Messenger used to send me his really bad poetry via the Net.

> *I am me, and he is he.*
> *My spirit is mine, and yours is thine*
> *And never the twain shall meet . . .*

Yes, really.

Then one day Messenger emailed me that he was giving up the Spiritual Quest, abandoning his Messenger persona and going back to his wife and two children in New Jersey. But in Peru at that time he was still Messenger. And he looked after Ryan in a gentle and loving way when they shared a room.

Most of our group stuck to their given names – Mary and Dian, Lorna and Alex, Jo and Sean, Jeanine and Jan. Things got a bit complicated when it came to Bunny. Bunny was her nickname – she'd been called Bunny since she was a child. She started to explain but was overcome with the giggles. Bunny was a remarkable lady. She had been married to a very wealthy mining magnate who had protected and cosseted her all her married life. So unworldly was she that she had never handled her own money and didn't know how to use a credit card. Although her grown-up children were against her travelling on her own now that she was a widow, Bunny was determined to make this journey to Bolivia and Peru.

'It's a dream I've had all my life,' she told me.

Then getting down to practicalities she asked, 'How much spending money do you think I should bring with me?'

'It depends . . .' I answered.

'Will 30 000 American dollars be enough?'

In Cusco's Plaza de Armas, its ancient and modern centre, which corresponds roughly to the ceremonial *huacapata*, the Incas' ancient central plaza, is Cusco's cathedral which sits solidly on the foundations of the Inca Viracocha's palace. The locals believe that an Indian chief is imprisoned in the cathedral's right-hand tower, awaiting the day when he can restore the glory of the Inca Empire. Here, too, hangs the huge miraculous gold-and-bronze bell of Maria Angola, named after a freed African slave girl and reputed to be one of the largest church bells in the world.

The cathedral, started in 1550 and only finished a century later, is built in the shape of a Latin cross and has a three-aisled nave supported by just fourteen massive pillars. One aisle is dominated by a floor-to-ceiling altar whose every inch is covered in gold leaf – pillars, paintings, frames. Statues of the Virgin Mary are everywhere, but all wear a doughily pale, complacent tight-lipped smirk. There's an altar of finely embossed silver and another of solid gold, heavy and geometric.

'The Black Jesus' (blackened by centuries of candle smoke) hangs over another altar. Legend has it that when a major earthquake shook the city in 1650 and the people took to the streets in terror, it was only when the Black Jesus was paraded through the Plaza de Armas that the tremors ceased.

I gaze at a large painting of The Last Supper, which at first looks totally traditional, in style and composition similar to the Da Vinci painting. Only when I look closely do I notice that the food is indigenous. In front of Christ is a large plate with a roasted guinea pig on it – a favourite staple diet of the Quechua. Whether the local mestizo artist sneaked the guinea pig in under the eyes of the ever-vigilant Catholic priests, or whether the Dominicans just turned a blind eye, we will never know.

The local craftsmen also showed their hand in other ways. The armrests of the finely carved wooden choir behind the altar are supported by pregnant-bellied carvings of Pachamama, the Inca Earth Goddess. And a number of other altars have painted carvings of Peruvian jungle fauna. The cathedral also has a superb collection of the Cusquena School of Art. All those hundreds of years ago the priests and Spanish artists taught the local Quechua artists to paint in the European way, even sending some of them to Europe to perfect their style and technique. There's a 'Renaissance' School, followed by a 'Flemish' School.

There's also a room full of very grand coats of arms given by the Spanish to the towns and villages they conquered and occupied. What a lesson in hubris, I think to myself.

We walk a couple of blocks down Avenida del Sol to Koricancha ('golden enclosure') where the Church of Santo Domingo rises from the walls of the ancient Temple of the Sun. Ironically, earthquakes have toppled parts of the church, but the superbly crafted Inca masonry has stood fast. Not only a temple, Koricancha was also an intricate celestial observatory where learned priests and astronomers plotted the solstices and equinoxes and predicted eclipses, all of which were intricately tied to sacred and agricultural practices.

We now know that the Koricancha was the centre of a geographical zodiac wheel that encompassed 327 sacred sites. Every summer solstice, the rays of the sun shine directly into the Tabernacle where only the Inca himself was allowed to sit. Covered with beaten gold and studded with emeralds and turquoise it must literally have dazzled the eyes when the sun shone. At the height of the Inca power, four small sanctuaries and a large temple were encircled by a cornice of gold, and below the temple was a garden in which everything was made from gold or silver and encrusted with precious jewels, from llamas and shepherds to snails and butterflies.

No wonder the Conquistadors were awed and made greedy by this magnificent complex; after all, gold was their motive for coming to the New World. By 1492 the Spanish had thrown out the Moors, thrown out the Jews, and now they were looking to explore what they called the New World. They claimed that they wanted to spread the word of Christianity, but they had heard that this New World was filled with gold. That's why their ships, with leaders such as Pizarro, set off from Spain.

How they tricked the Inca Emperor Atahuallpa after they promised him his freedom if he provided them with a room full of gold, how they looted Cusco's Temple of the Sun of some 1500 kilograms of pure gold, and how they later baptised Atahuallpa, said a credo for him and then strangled him, is now the stuff of history.

Two days later we are in the Amazon Basin, at a jungle lodge a few miles upstream from the tiny river port of Puerto Maldonado. We are to take part in an ayahuasca ceremony.

I am going to try to recreate the past.

10

Do you have to throw up to get to the Other Side?

Of course you can't recreate the past.
But I wanted to.

Two years before I had taken part in an ayahuasca ceremony in the Amazon Basin not far from where we are now, and I'd had a life-changing, transcendental experience. Today, Felipe, our shaman of the previous experience, is again to conduct the ceremony.

If you were me you would have done exactly the same thing.

But let me take you back to that first occasion, when Alan and I, along with a small group of fellow pilgrims, first drank the juice of the sacred vine, *Banisteriopsis caapi*.

Carol, also our group leader on that occasion, had told us that we could make a personal request of the spirits, that we could use this ceremony as an opportunity to ask the spirits, the divinity, whom or whatsoever, for something we think we need, to be cured, to learn something about our lives, their meaning and purpose. Whatever.

I did so and this is what happened to me.

It's two years ago.

We chug upstream from Puerto Maldonado for two hours or more. Finally, our canoe noses its way towards a high bank where steps carved out of the mud and edged with wooden poles lead up to a simple camp consisting of a few wooden huts on stilts, roofed with plaited palm leaves. Hundreds of small green parrots are nesting in holes in the high river bank, and as our canoe approaches, they rise up in a great, green chattering flock, wheel out over the surface of the river, and then fly towards the camp, where they perch in the tall trees and scold us noisily and excitedly.

There's a blood-red full moon on the Amazon. Later that night, we sit in a bare wooden cabin on the edge of a great river. After each drinking a tiny glass of ayahuasca, the sacred medicine of the Amazonian Indians, we sit silently for the next hour or so listening to Felipe as he sings, prays and blows smoke over us. He calls upon the Christian god, the spirits, the *apukuna* (the lords of the mountains), Pachamama, a whole pantheon of gods and goddesses to help and direct us. He is no longer Felipe from the Amazon jungle, but the shaman, the guide of souls, who can take leave of his body and cross over from the visible world to the invisible one, and take us with him too.

Reality disappears.

After watching a series of brightly coloured images flash in front of my eyes – a process which takes a couple of hours or more – I experience something quite different. I'll take you back to that moment.

Quite suddenly the images and colours vanish. I feel as if I've been given an electric shock. I can see nothing. I sit quite still. At once I am enveloped in a moment of perfect mental clarity. The feeling is so sharp, so crisp, so critical, so unutterably clear, that it's like being back in Antarctica where everything is so pure, so pristine, it's as if the world has just been made. I genuinely feel the scales fall from my eyes. I see who I am, my strengths, my weaknesses, my role in life. I see the strengths and weaknesses of my family and friends too, and the part that I play in their lives.

I think, 'Yes, this is it, this is my life's purpose.' .

I experience a total acceptance of who and what I am. I feel a great surge of self-respect, respect for life, respect for others. I sit frozen in time and space, all-seeing, all-knowing, very wise.

Then I am engulfed in a feeling of perfect love. I feel love all around me as a physical presence – the love of my family, my friends, everybody I know. And a divine love, a love over and beyond all that I know. I bask in this love, my soul stretches in this all-encompassing love and I am aware, for the first time in my life, of how lucky I am.

Then a feeling of such total peace enfolds me that I silently acknowledge, 'Yes, there is a Peace that passeth all understanding, and this is it.'

I am in touch with the divine.

There are no questions left, no cynicism, no doubt.

I am in a state of perfect happiness, acceptance and peace.

I am sublime.

My whole life has been leading up to this – this is my Everlasting Moment.

Now, wouldn't you have tried to recreate that moment?

Of course you would.

But let's fast forward to this second occasion. Our group is bigger, fourteen South Africans and six Americans.

Imagine the scene. Again it is full moon on the Amazon and

bright moonlight shines into the wooden 'temple' at the back of the lodge, nestled among vines, huge trees and creepers. A heady perfume from some exotic night-flowering plant charges the air. The 'temple' is an octagonal wooden structure roofed with palm fronds and with a wooden ramp leading up to the only door. It's been built since we were last here. We have been given rubber mats and have arranged them around the edges of the floor, heads to the wall, feet pointing into the centre. We've all brought the pillows from our huts as well. It's a bit of a crush but we manage to fit in. I sit next to Dolphin, beside the door – a grievous mistake, to sit by the door, as I am shortly to find out. We sit quietly, expectantly, a little nervously. A small, still voice has been nagging me all day: *don't do this.*

Felipe arrives looking exactly as he did two years ago. Faded jeans, a check shirt and grubby sneakers. Because of the large size of our group, he was to have brought a helper with him, but the helper has gone to tend a sick child. On the last occasion, there had been only seven of us, and Felipe had been able to give us his full attention. Again, the pink, viscous ayahuasca liquid is in a Coke bottle, two Coke bottles this time.

One by one, we kneel or crouch in front of Felipe and toss back the 'medicine'. As before, it tastes foul. Then the temple becomes quiet as we wait for the ayahuasca to take effect. It is only Felipe who breaks the rather nervous silence – praying, singing, chanting, blowing smoke as before.

Vera is the first to go. She starts screaming, drumming her little heels on the floor and shouting out, 'I'm so tired! I'm so-o tired!'

She works herself up into such frenzy that Felipe and Carol both go over to where she is lying on the floor. They spend minutes – hours? (time has already become very elastic and hazy) – tending to her. She is in her element – the centre of attention. It's very hard to stay focused with such a racket going on, although Sybil, one of the young American girls, is sitting, eyes closed, with a beatific expression on her face. At last Vera ·gives one final piercing scream and, thankfully, passes out. As Carol and Felipe drag her inert, semi-upright body past me on its way to the door, I see her little patent leather boots trailing along behind her on the wooden floor. She disappears into the noises of the night – the river rushing, frogs and toads croaking, strange night birds calling, the grunting of some small animals as they rustle in the bushes.

Bunny stands up. Lovely, gracious, fragile, ladylike Bunny – and totters to the door. She just makes it on to the ramp, where she leans over, politely throws up, and totters back to her place facing me on the far side of the wooden room. She lies down and goes to sleep. Paul is lying beside her and is the next to go. One hundred kilograms of human 'bear' lurch heavily across the floor and stumble through the door, retching and groaning loud enough to wake the dead. He, too, just makes it to the railing outside the door and vomits thunderously over the side. Then, after what seems, minutes, hours, days (I am getting more and more woozy), he lurches back to his place, misses his footing and crashes down on Bunny's sleeping form. She doesn't stir.

The next day Bunny tells me how caring and concerned Paul had been about her.

'Even though I was sleeping, I could hear him asking me if I was all right. Was there anything he could do for me? So sweet and thoughtful.'

As well he might. *He* tells me the next day that when he crashed down on her he thought he had killed her, hence his concern.

Ryan is next, but is not sick. He makes it to the ramp, lies across it like a stranded starfish, and sings quietly to himself in a terrible off-key voice. Vera is laid out at the bottom of the ramp under the full moon in her Tutankhamun-like death pose.

Rob, one of the Americans, leaves the temple and starts baying the moon like an overactive werewolf. His howls finally subside into human noises – terror, sorrow, regret, apologies.

'I'm sorry! I'm sorry,' he sobs over and over again.

Vera rises from the dead and goes to sit beside Ryan.

'I love you, Ryan. You are so beautiful.'

Ryan sings on tunelessly.

Sybil sits quietly throughout all this physical and emotional tumult with a serene, composed expression on her face. The next day she tells me she had 'the most wonderful experience', was oblivious to everything going on around her, and felt that she 'was the Universe'. Jan also, had a memorable, warm experience. He felt he was inside a beautiful bubble of pink and blue that was shining its light on the world.

Sean, also a member of our South African group, is sitting on the floor on the other side of the room with Mary and Dian, the sisters-in-law, next to Bunny and Paul. Over six feet tall, with blond curly hair and wide blue eyes, he has just sold his extremely successful IT business, and is taking time out to 'find himself'. Hence this trip to Peru.

I amble over to them. Sean looks up at me with big blue eyes wide and stricken, and without a trace of irony asks, 'Do you have to throw up to get to the Other Side?'

I go back to my place next to Dolphin and we huddle together giggling. Carol warns us to be quiet.

To be quiet! When all this howling, and singing, and baying, and people throwing up is going on! We giggle even harder.

Now it's my turn. I rush outside, throw up over the railing and find Dian smoking a cigarette beside me. We chat meaningfully about nothing at all.

Suddenly a herd of cows floats past in the jungle. They are real cows even if their gait seems strange. I notice Alan in the middle of them. He kneels down, is sick, and looks up to find a herd of cows staring at him sympathetically.

Messenger pads up the wooden ramp from somewhere in the jungle and comes up to me. He adopts a Wise-Guru mode and tries to counsel me.

'If you have baggage,' he tells me solemnly, 'now is the time to get rid of it. You can confide in me.'

He hiccups quietly.

Thanks, but no thanks, I tell him.

He then tries Alan who has somehow made it back to the ramp from his bovine get-together.

'Everybody,' intones Messenger sonorously, catching hold of Alan's arm, 'has something to throw away.'

Hiccup.

'Fancy!' says Alan, lurching off again into the night.

Except for Sybil and Jan, the whole evening was a rout – an unmitigated disaster. Whether Felipe had changed his ayahuasca recipe, whether the omens were not auspicious, whether the vibes were wrong, whether Felipe's missing helper could indeed have helped, whether we weren't spiritually ready, whether the spirits weren't ready, we will never know. In retrospect, I wouldn't have missed the experience for anything, although at the time it was a cross between a tragedy and a comedy, like being caught in the middle of a bad dream that has its funny moments too.

Apart from Jeanine, who was still lying quietly at the back of the temple, thinking about this and that, but always very much in the present reality, Bunny and Alan were almost the last to leave. They walked along the jungle paths for hours discussing Life, Death, the Hereafter, Karma, Kismet, Predestination and Free Will, and The Meaning of Life. When they finally stopped to say goodnight, they found they had walked only about 20 metres from the temple.

The next day we walk with our guide Antonio deep into the forest and watch butterflies, beetles and birds. We hear the piercing call of a toucan. And become grounded in the present.

No, you can't recreate the past, but it was worth a try. And I learned a hell of a lot in the process.

We fly back to Cusco, and from our base at Willka T'ika, Carol's lovely ranch in the Sacred Valley of the Incas, we visit Pisaq. Pisaq is a delightful little market town in the Urubamba Valley, built round a square whose cobbles were laid by the Spaniards over four hundred years ago. Mountains cradle the town and fluffy white clouds skim over the huge tree outside the small church on the west side of the square.

But today we are not here to browse amongst the colourful stalls of Pisaq's legendary market, we are here to climb up to Pisaq's Temple of the Sun. We scramble up a very steep route not often used by tourists. From a high vantage point we can see the Temple. It lies as if in a cupped hand, open to the sun. Through a rocky tunnel, up and down stone steps, past crumbling stone walls, we make our way down to the Temple.

We have taken it in turns to lead Ryan. Today Mary is with him, keeping well back from the main party and proceeding very slowly and carefully. We did not make a roster or any plan, we just naturally took our turn to walk arm in arm with him, help him, guide him, dress him and cut up his food for him. As Mary had predicted, it was an enriching experience for all of us. We saw things through his inner eyes, heard sounds that we might have missed, touched things that we might have overlooked.

Alex, a dynamic young member of our group, and also a very successful businessman like Sean, happens to be at the front of the group this day. I am just behind him as we slither and slip, stumble and balance along the very uneven, rocky path. Alex is going helter-skelter, determined to reach the Temple first. Suddenly, he stops dead in his tracks.

'Who is with Ryan today?' he asks me.

'Mary.'

'She's not big enough and strong enough to handle this.'

Alex disappears. We sit down beside the path and wait.

Some minutes later Alex reappears with Ryan on his back. They pass us and make their way down to the Temple. It is a touching moment and one I will never forget.

We all sit quietly in The Temple of the Sun. In the midst of these high ruins is a huge, shaped and chiselled rock, the *Chakana* stone, similar to the 'Hitching Post of the Sun' in Machu Picchu. The Incas believed these great stones connected humans to the heavens. It was from this point that the ancient astronomers monitored the stars and measured the solstices, gauging exactly when to sow and when to reap. Terraces, centuries-old, step up almost to the mountain peaks, their irrigation systems still functional. Quechua farmers still cultivate their crops on these Inca terraces, practising crop rotation each year.

I've been supercharged with energy today. Now I sit in the

sun and meditate, feeling golden and peaceful.

Suddenly a local Spanish Guide from Hell arrives, a red-headed harpy with a shrieking voice, conducting four German tourists round the site. Her shrieking disturbs all of us and shatters the tranquillity of the morning. I ask her very politely, *por favor*, to be a little quieter. A stream of abuse is heaped on my head. She then finds Carol guiding Ryan's hands over the Chakana and goes ballistic.

'It is forbidden to touch this stone!'

Carol tries to explain, but the harpy gets more and more hysterical. Vera glances at her admiringly.

Later we hear from one of the local drivers that they are all ashamed of this particular local guide. They apologise to Carol.

'She's been in Germany too long,' mutters an old driver.

Back at Willka T'ika Ryan decides to practise psychic surgery on Mary, who had slipped after the ayahuasca fiasco and cut her head. He is so gentle and persuasive that Mary feels she can't refuse. So Ryan 'operates'.

First he places a 'crystal' (invisible because it's psychic) in the middle of Mary's forehead to anaesthetise her. Then, using another psychic crystal he 'cuts' into her head and clamps the wound open with more crystals. He then 'bores' a hole into her skull until he can see the cerebrospinal fluid, removes the wound and the scar tissue by suctioning them out with yet another crystal, then sutures her up again with crystal scissors. He then takes a golden bandage and binds Mary up.

'How do you feel?' I ask Mary.

'Fine.'

We visit Machu Picchu and I find it as fascinating and awe-inspiring as I had the first time. I could go back again and again.

On our last night we have a party at Willka T'ika. We dance and sing and relive our Bolivian and Peruvian experiences – both good and bad – over and over again. Bunny gets up from where she is reclining on some cushions on the floor and does a feisty, mock strip to Pan pipes. It is an incredibly happy evening.

Six months after we got back to South Africa, Bunny died. But she had done what she wanted to and fulfilled her lifetime dream to visit Peru.

And Vera?

I have never seen or heard of her again.

11

The Wonder Of It . . .

I'm sometimes asked, 'Have you ever lost your sense of wonder?'

Never!

Ever since I was a child I have related deeply to the earth and to the natural world. I found meaning and wonder in the first thrilling call of the cuckoo in Spring, or in watching Doris put out a saucer of milk for the hedgehogs that came up from the wild wood at the back of our home, or when I searched with Rita along the banks of an old railway cutting for the first violets and primroses, or watched a robin redbreast singing his cheery little song as he sat on the handle of my father's spade when the snow lay deep over the garden.

When I first came to southern Africa, over thirty years ago, a whole new natural world opened up to me. As a travel writer I've since travelled far and wide in Sub-Saharan Africa, and will continue to do so. I would like to believe, as the San hunter-gatherers of the great Kalahari Desert do, that after I die my spirit will go up into the heavens with all the other departed souls, become a star, and shine down on earth and my loved ones, for ever and ever.

In the far north of Botswana is the great, starkly beautiful, bare region of Savute. Here is a river channel parched by two decades of drought, a mysteriously dry river channel that last flowed twenty years ago, but to which game still flocks in great numbers. Once the lifeline of the area, this wide channel – the Savute Channel – is Africa's Stolen River of myth and legend. It's a place of open spaces, limitless horizons, wide skies and unending miles of tall, waving yellow grass dotted with dramatically beautiful dead trees – the legacy of the relentless drought.

In summertime, thousands of migrating plains animals – zebra and wildebeest – provide prey for powerful lion prides (some numbering over thirty), scavenging hyenas, and the graceful, swift cheetah that follow the herds. But it's for elephants, one of Africa's largest concentrations of elephants, that the Savute region is perhaps best known.

It's winter, about eight o'clock at night. I'm sitting alone on the wooden veranda outside my tented chalet in Savute Elephant Camp. The chalet is built up on stilts overlooking the camp's waterhole. I'm looking out on bare white sand, twisted dead trees silhouetted against the skyline, a few ancient old living trees framing the opposite bank of the dry riverbed. Thousands of glittering stars are pinning up the sky and there's a three-quarter orange moon illuminating the heavens. Sshhh! The elephants are coming to drink! The great bull elephants of Savute.

Come and watch with me.

Great, grey, ghostly shapes come and go, break into little runs as they near the water, emerging out of the darkness like huge phantoms. They observe an unknown elephant discipline

– unknown to humans, that is – a little-understood pachyderm protocol. But each elephant knows the rules. It waits its turn in disciplined fashion, because the waterhole is narrow and tiny, only a few feet long, so that only two or three elephants can drink at a time.

They greet and grumble, jostle politely for space, wade, slurp, slop, squelch and suck. Great gulping sounds and gurgles fill the night air. And overall, loud purring sounds rumble and grumble, vibrate and drone – like the purring of contented giant cats – the elephants' communication system. Trunks intertwine, caress, prod or search. Some elephants stand with their trunks looped over their tusks, having a momentary rest from the action. Sometimes a gigantic bellow fills the night as an older patriarch reminds the youngsters of their lesser place in the scheme of things. Elephants back off, retreat at the warning raised trunks of others, move forward again, are re-challenged, wait, gain another pace or two, imperceptibly edging closer to the water.

The passing parade continues. Some elephants stand motionless, some shift softly from great foot to great foot, some back off from one another, retreating a few steps before attempting another few steps towards the cool, fresh water. There's gentle jostling, grouping and regrouping. Moths flit by, lit white by the lights of the camp. The elephants continue to come and go. There's a still, dignified, almost elegant ambience amongst the great beasts. The air is pungent with their smell, mixed with the fragrant scent of wood smoke and wild sage.

Look at the tusks! Big heavy ones, little short stumpy ones, long thin ones and broken ones. One old elephant has no tusks at all. One by one, after each has drunk, and sometimes it takes many, many minutes for an elephant to drink his fill, each huge grey shape wanders off into the night. One elephant has forgotten how to move. He stands motionless to one side of the gently moving, pulsating mass, frozen like a gigantic granite statue. Utterly still. Only his eyelashes flick from time to time. The cry of a hyena punctuates the air, and in the distance a lion is calling.

And still the elephants keep coming. Now a mother and baby approach with a few teenage elephants. What will the great bulls do? They allow the youngsters to pass through their midst to drink. The tiny baby gets special treatment. He is allowed to kneel down at the edge of the deep hole and drink his fill. He hasn't yet learned how to use his trunk, so slurps water up into his mouth. Two big giants don't quite notice him and press against his tiny form. The baby emits an indignant squeal of protest, and the biggest bull of all cautions the careless adults with a loud trumpet and a strong push. Baby Alert! Be more careful! Take more care!

As the throng continues to shift and move, a huge bull elephant materialises from the darkness and marches confidently towards the mass of heaving grey bodies. The others fall back respectfully as he strides straight to the water source and drinks his fill. No uncertainty here about the hierarchy.

Elephants. Moving. Shifting. Dancing a slow pavane under a now dark sky rich with a million stars. And still they keep coming . . . two legs at a time, one side then the other, the slow measured paces of treading down centuries of evolution. And still they keep coming . . . emerging from the shadows, becoming more substantial as they near the water.

These are the great elephants of Savute.

Botswana is one of my favourite places on earth – a place to reflect, a place to wonder, a place of dramatically different landscapes and terrains. There's the water wilderness of the Okavango Delta, formed by the Okavango River that flows down from the Angolan highlands and fans out over north-western Botswana. It's made up of an intricate network of narrow channels and crystal-clear lagoons, backwaters lined with papyrus and reeds – the haunt of huge crocodiles and snorting hippos where water lilies float on the shimmering surfaces and scores of different birds make their home.

I once saw three lions swimming across from one island to another, shaking themselves once safely on shore, thousands of water drops scattering like crystals in the noonday sun. Another time on Chief's Island I walked into two lions having a territorial dispute. So involved were they with their roaring and pouncing, advancing and retreating, that they didn't notice me. My guide and I stood stock still until the dominant resident lion had chased the young nomad intruder away. On another occasion, walking from a lodge to my tent, I was confronted by a very large hyena.

'Shoo!' I said in my fiercest voice, raising my arms above my head. I couldn't think of anything else to say.

And shoo it did, slinking away hurriedly into the African night.

Another place of striking beauty, unlike anywhere else in Botswana – maybe even in Africa – is the Makgadikgadi Pans.

It's the end of winter. Outside my tent hangs a green canvas washstand. It swings to and fro in the light wind that whispers across the seemingly limitless plains of yellow grass. The dry fronds of the tall palms that stand sentinel to the camp rustle and creak. The melancholy croaks of the huge Pied Crows that unceasingly patrol the area are the only other sounds.

In the washstand's tiny mirror I watch as the savannah, the small bare trees and scrubby bushes, and a line of palm trees marching across the distant horizon dance, vanish and reappear in the shimmering heat waves. For me, these shifting reflections symbolise the unreal, almost illusory nature of this place, a place where nothing is quite as it seems, where so often it is almost impossible to distinguish between reality and illusion.

Once upon a time, about two million years ago, a huge lake – the largest in the world – stretched over most of Botswana. This super-lake filled much of the Kalahari Basin and was fed by three of Africa's mightiest rivers, the Okavango, the Zambezi and the Chobe. Together, scientists conjecture, they flowed across the Kalahari Desert, met the Limpopo, and finally found their collective way to the Indian Ocean. In its heyday this lake was possibly as much as 100 metres deep. But then, over the millennia, geological shifts (for this was a tectonically unstable area), climatic changes, erosion and silting, pushed back the great rivers that fed the lake, and it gradually became smaller, dwindling aeon after aeon until it dried up into the immense salt pans that remain today. Astronauts have observed the outlines of these ancient shorelines from space – although the levels fluctuated, they stayed long enough to mark their existence. Covering an area of some 12 000 square kilometres, the shallow pans are seasonal. In the summer months, after the first rains, they fill up with water, and fresh grass grows. Then thousands upon thousands of zebra and wildebeest, often stalked by lions and other predators, come to eat and drink their fill. Huge flocks of flamingos, pelicans and other water birds move in and, for a few short months, the pans live again.

But it was winter when I once made an extraordinary journey across these pans.

Our small party of six has just spent a night at San camp, a tented camp some 50 kilometres south of Gweta, and now we are to cross the legendary open spaces of the dry pans on quad bikes. I'm excited and exhilarated although I'm told it is an arduous three-day trip. We will camp on the mystical, magical, starkly beautiful Kubu Island, which rises 20 metres above the surrounding pancake-flat surfaces that stretch to the horizon and beyond in the south-west corner of Sowa Pan. Mike, our guide, has told us that Kubu Island is one of the remotest corners of the world, unparalleled for its peace, isolation and silence.

After a brief lecture on the ways and whimsies of quad bikes, we set out eastwards into the unknown in single formation. Mike rides alone, the rest of us two per bike – we shall take it in turns to drive. Adolf, the other guide and bike mechanic, brings up the rear.

We wear brightly coloured cotton scarves – Lawrence of Arabia style – wrapped tightly round our heads to protect us from the white dust and heat. As we penetrate deeper and deeper into the pans, the vegetation diminishes from tall, graceful palms, which grow furthest from the pans (the legacy of palm nut-eating elephants who roamed this way in times gone by), to smaller trees, then bushes and shrubs, the ubiquitous salt grasses and then – nothing. The last vestige of growth we see before the immense whiteness of the pans takes over, is a brave little salt bush, struggling to survive until the first rains come. In the middle of the bush, amazingly, is an owl pellet.

Finally Mike says, 'Welcome to the middle of nowhere!'

And he is right. There is not a blade of grass, not a tree, not a stone. Just the unending expanse of a white pan, in the middle of what was once Africa's super-lake. It's a piecrust surface of hard, salt-saturated clay. But, beware – the hardness is only crust deep. Ride off the single track and you could sink deep into the moisture that lies just below the surface.

Some of the surface flakes are as big as a squashed rhinoceros; others the size of dinner plates; still smaller ones are saucer-sized.

We stop every thirty minutes or so to stretch our legs, reapply sun-block, drink as much water as we can hold, and to seek out miniature treasures – the tiny shells of freshwater crabs, 'earstones' of fishes from a distant past – evidence that this was once a huge, freshwater lake. We look at them closely, wonder, and then return them to the pan.

As we press on through this great place of flaky nothingness under the pitiless sun and blinding whiteness, mirages on the horizon dance, tantalise and dazzle the senses. Look! There's an island of palm trees surrounded by a blue lake! There's a clump of verdant, leafy trees! We ride further and further into the heart of the pan and, suddenly, in front of us and all around us, is the ocean – with rolling white breakers foaming on to sandy shores. The illusion is so real and compelling we feel we could run into the cool, inviting waves, so seductive in the bone dryness of the pans. This 'sea' continues to taunt and tease us for kilometres.

We stop to eat our sandwiches, huddling in the small pools of shade offered by the quads' wheels. Then on again, over bumpy mounds, navigating ridges, furrows and aardvark holes, always eastward. A couple of hours before sunset, we see in the far distance a tree-covered bump that looks just like a sleeping hippo ('kubu' means hippo in Setswana).

'Kubu Island . . .' breathes Mike proudly. 'Welcome to the

most beautiful place on earth.'

It certainly doesn't look like much from a distance, but as we draw nearer we begin to make out the huge granite boulders, the smooth, round pebbles formed by the rolling waters of the prehistoric lake, and the oddly shaped, giant – but somehow stunted-looking – baobab trees, and we begin to appreciate Mike's enthusiasm. The red, pink and purple baobabs, gnarled and twisted as they are, bespeak centuries of struggle against this harsh, unforgiving terrain. They keep silent vigil over grey boulders spattered with white, fossilised guano and red and orange lichen, and clumps of bright yellow grass. It's as if the brush of a larger-than-life Impressionist painter has splashed all the colours about in a moment of creative abandon.

We drive slowly round the island in the last rays of the setting sun. The magical, fairy-tale properties of the baobabs are the stuff of African legend. And indeed, this is a holy and sacred place to the San people. When a few of the staff from San Camp had arrived earlier by truck with the camping gear, they noticed an irritating small wind threatening to blow up into a sandstorm. One of the San, a tiny, wizened old tracker who hardly reached my shoulder, told me he had said a quick prayer to the spirits of the place and the wind soon dropped.

We're very weary. We each find a silent and solitary spot to rest and soak up the ambience. As the sun sets, the lone and level salt pans stretch far away. That night, under a sky brilliantly thick with stars, I believe – like the San – that I can hear the stars sing. Not so much a song as a celestial choral symphony. In the middle of the night, lying on a mattress under this brilliant canopy, I see the tails of two shooting stars blaze across the Milky Way and explode in a shower of heavenly sparks like a giant firework.

Up at dawn for the wondrous sight of the first rays of the sun striking the baobabs. After walking round the island and examining the dry stone walls of an ancient settlement – where we find Stone Age cutting tools and shards of pottery at least two thousand years old – we ride our bikes to an ancient, pebbled and rocky shoreline, which marks a former outer perimeter of the pan. In the pulsing afternoon heat, we climb 150 metres to its ridge, and find thousand-year-old San beads of ostrich egg, ivory and bone, and more pieces of patterned, earth-red and terracotta-coloured pottery. On his last trip, Mike found two blue glass trading beads here – this was once an old trading route. Here, too, are more centuries-old stone walls.

The view from the top of the ridge is breathtaking. A great white nothingness shimmering in the heat as far as our dazzled eyes can see. On the way back to Kubu Island we stop to wander on foot over the pan's salty, crisp surfaces and discover more treasures – a crystallised lark, a crystallised moth and several crystallised grasshoppers; a desert rat frozen in salty time, and the small, pink downy feather of a flamingo chick.

That night the new moon glows yellow under the stars.

Southern Africa is blessed with a rare and unique beauty. Let me take you now to Namibia.

Namibia is often called 'The Land God Made in Anger' because of its stark, surreal landscapes, untamed wilderness and harsh environment. But those ancient San gods knew what they doing when they created Namibia. I believe they were so pleased with their creation that they decided never to replicate it, because Namibia is like no place else on earth.

You can't beat deserts for inspiring a sense of wonder. I count myself very, very lucky because I've experienced many of earth's great deserts. I've sipped mint tea in a Bedouin tent in the Arabian Desert, slept under the stars in the Sahara, flown over Australia's Red Heart and then climbed its monolithic mile-high natural monument, Uluru, formerly called Ayers Rock. I've gazed at some of the greatest wonders of the ancient world in the Egyptian desert and raced a camel in the great Desert of Thar in India's north-west Rajasthan province, just 80 kilometres from the Pakistan border. I've marvelled at the snow and ice deserts in Antarctica and heard the stars sing – as the San people say they do – in the Kalahari. And I've seen one of Nature's most dazzling desert firework displays – the Namaqualand daisies in the Karoo. But two of my favourite deserts are both in Namibia – Damaraland, and the world's oldest living desert, the Namib. I have marvelled at the majesty of these deserts and my soul has revived there.

Damaraland, situated in north-west Namibia, is a desert of a very different kind to the classic sand dunes of the Namib. It's a landscape of almost unsurpassed rugged beauty formed by millions of years of unending geological movement. Vivid brick-red sediments complement grey lava slopes punctuated by black fingers of 'frozen' basaltic rock creeping down from the jagged rocky horizons. Millions and millions of stones, great, small, tiny, interspersed with clumps of silvery-grey shrubs and pioneer grasses litter the unending slopes, hillsides and mountain faces.

There seem to be as many rocks, huge and small, in Damaraland as there are grains of sand on the beaches of the windswept, treacherous Skeleton Coast, some 90 kilometres to the west. But there is life – and plenty of it – in this seemingly inhospitable landscape. From my tent, I walk up a steep stony hill to look at dozens of *Welwitschia mirabilis* – reputed to be the world's longest-living plants – that can live up to a thousand years. As I stop at a 500-year-old 'youngster', I notice a newborn Cape hare sheltering under one of its shiny, long green leaves.

I think to myself that when this plant was the same age as this tiny furry creature, Columbus was sailing for the New World. More or less at the same time, a daring little band of Portuguese sailors, inspired by the vision of their charismatic leader, Prince Henry the Navigator (who surprisingly never left his native land), was setting sail from the School of Navigation at Sagres, the most western point of Europe, to find fame, fortune and new lands for the Crown. Facing unknown dangers and *terra incognita* (the maps of the time were little more than fanciful sketchbooks filled with dragons and legends like 'here be monsters'), nautical mile by nautical mile these intrepid sailors pushed back the edges of the known world until they entered the waters of the south-west coastline of Africa – known today as Namibia.

In 1485, Captain Diego Cão and his battered crew finally dropped anchor off a desolate beach thousands of kilometres from home and safety. There on the windswept beach, they erected a cross both in honour of the Divine King who had protected and directed them during their arduous journey, as well as King John I, their earthly monarch.

North of the little seaside town of Swakopmund there's a replica of that cross on a little rise overlooking thousands upon thousands of Cape fur seals at Cape Cross.

Further north is the notorious Skeleton Coast. The Portuguese, facing the crashing seas of this icy coast in their tiny, frail caravels, called it the Coast of Death. Littered with innumerable shipwrecks, bleached whalebones, and scavenged by marauding jackals and sea birds, this part of Namibia is testament to the puny and transient insignificance of humankind.

But today I'm in Damaraland watching a newborn Cape hare. All around are colourful lichen fields, dark-green, umbrella-shaped camelthorn trees, candelabra euphorbias raising their prickly fleshy arms to the cloudless sky, salt bushes and the ubiquitous Shepherd's Tree. I sit on the rough ground and listen to the silence.

That night we drive in a chill desert wind coming off the Atlantic through the rocky desert rubble to Slangpost, a small verdant oasis in the middle of what seems to be nowhere (not even the mountains have a name in this part of the world and are known simply as the 'no-name' mountains). We see the first traces of the amazing Desert Elephants, their huge footprints trodden over by the healthy herds of goats and sheep belonging to the local Damara farmers. It's a bizarre sight and a bizarre concept – elephants and goats, pachyderms and people. The next day we come very close to a small herd of Desert Elephants along the surprisingly green and fertile dry Huab River bed. They exist by browsing on the large seed pods of the Ana tree and whatever else they find edible. They stand up on their long hind legs and pull at the branches to get at the pods. To see the great grey shapes silhouetted against the sandy mounds of the dry river, ringed by mountains and sand dunes, is an unforgettable sight. Another day I see them plodding over a high, stony mountain, bent on some ancient ancestral errand.

In a spectacular fiery dawn I marvel at a moringa tree – the 'enchanted' tree – so-called because according to San legend, the God of Thunder didn't want moringa trees in Paradise, so he pulled them all up and threw them out. They fell upside down into the earth and remind me of miniature baobab trees.

A flock of Greybacked Finchlarks blows through its branches like a bunch of dry leaves. A Longbilled Lark picks about at my feet and dapper black and white Mountain Chats fly hither and thither scolding the camp cat which is unsuccessfully trying to creep up on them. The wind whistles softly and eerily through the moon-like landscape.

But for a desert that fulfils all my romantic notions of what a *real* desert should look like (my imagination fuelled by movies such as *Lawrence of Arabia* and *The English Patient*), then you can't beat Namibia's Namib Desert – the world's oldest, living desert where mighty sand dunes roar, rumble and wander.

Sossusvlei is one of the most remarkable sights in the Namib-Naukluft Park, one of the biggest nature reserves in Africa. Huge towering dunes, said to be the highest in the world, rise dramatically over a thousand metres above the surrounding plains. I'm staying at a camp, surely one of the most dramatically sited in Africa, of nine thatched chalets perched on a mountainside, looking out into the distance towards the faraway mountains over seemingly endless flat, yellow plains. The profound silence is broken only by the calls of the Barking Geckos as they chatter to each other in the falling light.

The towering, sculpted dunes of Sossusvlei are unique. There are the crescent-shaped barchan dunes that migrate up to two or three metres a year, covering and uncovering whatever crosses their path. There are the fossil dunes that consist of ancient sand that solidified millions of years ago. Then there are the spectacular star-shaped dunes, formed by the multi-directional winds that tease and tumble the sands back and forth. At dawn, the dunes change colour from palest pink and soft yellow, to a deeper coral, then rose-red, ochre, russet and finally, blood-red. I climb, puffing and panting (but it's worth every laboured breath) to the top of 'Big Daddy', the highest sand dune in the world and gaze at a landscape so surreal and awe-inspiring that I'm humbled. I feel my mortality, kneading the bones under the flesh of my face, and think that humans are nothing compared to this vastness.

On the way down I rest at Dead Vlei – a white pan punctuated with the black fingers of dead trees – and then make my leisurely way to the bottom of the dunes where I sit in the shade of the camelthorn trees. I watch the bird life, and then focus my binoculars on distant climbers still struggling up Big Daddy. I've sipped sundowners in this desert, gone hot air ballooning at dawn over the dunes, and marvelled at the life contained in this harsh environment – not Big Game, but a wealth of bird and insect 'specials', as well as unique plants and geological formations.

Where there are dunes, there are some of the world's strangest, desert-adapted creatures. There are sun-bathing beetles that collect condensed drops of moisture on their backs which they then roll down to their mouths, and there are other beetles that dig trenches to collect moisture. The Golden Mole (once thought to be extinct) spends its life 'swimming' under the dunes, popping up to the surface to grab unwary insects. The Side-winding Adder does just that – winds itself from side to side as it makes its way over the sand – and there's a sand-diving lizard that stands motionless, one foot raised, as if in some ancient ritual dance.

I've sat alone in this desert and listened to the silence – soul-searing, soul-searching, thunderous silence where, if you listen hard, you can hear the language of another world.

No, I have never lost my sense of wonder.

On the fifth of July 2001 I was with my dear friend Sylvia, also a journalist and travel writer, in the Okavango Delta in Botswana. We often travel together and have seen much, experienced much, laughed and wept together, shared each other's joys and tragedies. On this particular night we were at Duba Plains, one of the Okavango Delta's most remote camps. Built on an island shaded by large ebony, fig and garcinia trees and surrounded by flood plains which are seasonally flooded, the camp is located in the furthermost reaches of the Delta.

We had flown in earlier that day in one of the little planes that service these Delta camps which are inaccessible by road. Duba Plains is a very private reserve and is famous for probably the highest concentration of lion anywhere in Africa and some huge herds of buffalo. The plains stretch away forever in front of this tiny, intimate camp deep, deep in the Delta. It's wintertime, and we are almost marooned on an island surrounded by teeming wildlife. This July, so much water has come down into the Delta from the Angola Highlands that the animals are competing with the camps and their human inhabitants for dry land.

A pride of lions criss-crosses the camp once or twice a day, and Rancid, the camp hyena, is a familiar figure after dusk as he goes to check out what the kitchen can offer in the way of scraps. This evening Sylvia and I and our Motswana guide Sele have been out on the plains in an open Land Rover. The game drive has been spectacular, even in our rich bush experience. We have seen a pair of post-coital leopards dozing in the fading rays of the sun. We have watched a huge, old, black-maned lion continually mount and mate with a young lioness every three minutes or so, for so long that we voyeurs became weary of watching. We happened upon a herd of hundreds of muddy buffalo munching contentedly at the edge of a water meadow, and watched five young hyena cubs playing outside their den and then rushing to feed from mother as she returned from a hunting trip. We have been mock-charged by an elephant bull, and been dazzled by the evening antics of hundreds of water birds. When we arrive back in camp, full of wonder and joy, the camp managers Tania and James are waiting for us as the open Land Rover sloshes up through the water surrounding the camp. Tania throws her arms around me.

'You have a new grandson – Nicholas.'

I went quietly to my tent and wrote this letter to Nicholas, Tara and Mike's son, to be given to him when he is old enough to understand and to experience his own sense of wonder at Africa's bush.

My dear Nicholas

As you were being born in the historic old mining town of Kimberley, I was in the middle of the Okavango Delta, deep in the heart of Botswana. All the signs were auspicious at your birth. It was a gleaming, mystical, blood-red full moon, and as you entered the world, I was watching two of earth's loveliest creatures – a male and female leopard. He was at the base of an ancient jackalberry tree, she was stretched out on a thick branch above his head. I gazed deep into their green eyes and a moment of perfect recognition took place. It was almost as if they were sending me some kind of signal. I sense that you will be a very special person.

I offer you this night as a birthday present.

Dear child, may you have happiness and fulfilment, and may you also come to know the wonders of nature and the inter-connectedness of all things.

With love, Granny Kate

Later that night Sylvia and I went out into the Delta in a mokoro, a dugout canoe. We drifted along the papyrus-lined channels and finally were poled into a stretch of open water where the purple night water lilies perfumed the air and the reflection of the moon splintered on the soft waves made by the slowly moving mokoro. We clinked glasses of champagne together under that great blood-red moon, threw back our heads and whooped and chortled with joy.

> *And hand in hand, on the edge of the sand,*
> *We danced by the light of the moon,*
>> *The moon,*
>> *The moon,*
> *We danced by the light of the moon.*

Just like the Owl and the Pussycat.

12

The Lotus Flower

Life is full of new beginnings. The birth of Nicholas was only one.

When I left West Africa to go to Ireland I left a lot of things and a lot of people behind. I left a happy home, the teaching work I loved, my dogs and cats, my garden, Bassey my cook and Patrick my steward (who had now been with me for seven years), and Africa, which I had learned to love with a deep passion. And I left Malcolm.

The city of Derry began as a Celtic holy place and later became the site of a monastery founded by St Columcille in the sixth century. In the early 1600s Oliver Cromwell (he of the wart on his nose) started a project of 'planting' Ireland with Protestants and was most successful in Ulster. Adventurers, ex-soldiers, ne'er-do-wells and almost anybody else who was not Catholic but had the gift of the gab, managed to grab a piece of land in Northern Ireland. Derry itself was granted to the English guilds

(I once dined off gold plate in Derry's Guildhall) and was renamed 'Londonderry' to assert its new Anglo-Irish identity. To this day, I have never heard a local speak of anything but 'Derry'.

Derry is encircled by ancient city walls, 18 feet high and 20 feet thick, that were first erected nearly four hundred years ago. These mighty walls have never been breached and that's why the locals call Derry 'The Maiden City'. Apparently in the nineteenth century the fine ladies of Derry used to send to England for the latest fashions which, when they arrived from London, would be immediately donned by the well-padded forms of the English matrons, and paraded along the stout city walls. This so incensed the poor ragged Catholics who watched them from underneath the walls that they wrote indignant letters to the London newspapers, complaining about these parading 'cats'. The press ran with the nickname and that's how the fashion 'catwalks' of today got their name.

But all of this I was to find out much later.

In Ireland I was plunged into a totally new life. We lived first in a seedy flat in the heart of Derry's old town. It had three small rooms, an unspeakable little greasy kitchen and an even more depressing bathroom. Damp ran down the walls and black crows patrolled the roofs. It was an upstairs flat above a cycle shop in Sackville Street. There was no garden and so I strung a piece of twine outside the window to the neighbouring window opposite on which to hang the washing. Doris, back in England for a short while, was alarmed and unsettled by my behaviour (she loved Malcolm) and caught the next ferry over the Irish Sea to see what her younger, usually level-headed daughter was up to. And to check out Alan.

I watched Doris take in the miserable circumstances, the rainy weather, the overcast skies, and the children's chapped hands and faces. They were used to sunshine, heat and space, and found it difficult to be bundled up in scratchy duffel coats, Wellington boots and gloves. But they forgot their cold noses, chilblains and their swimming pool when they turned on the television set. Television was an absolute unknown in their previous life and now they were caught up in the fantasy world of Andy Pandy, Bill and Ben, the Flowerpot Men, and The Magic Roundabout.

Alan decided to resign his commission and leave the army.

'We'll move from here,' he promised me.

And then suddenly it was summer and the sun came out. We drove our old blue car out to the beaches of Donegal, down to Sligo and Connemara in the west of Ireland, explored the Antrim Coast Road (one of the most beautiful scenic coast roads in the world), clambered over the Giant's Causeway in the far north, and picnicked in old stone castles with names like Skattrick and Dunluce.

We visited Alan's birthplace, Omagh in County Tyrone, dominated by a range of mist-shrouded mountains covered with pine-scented forests. In late August we visited Northern Ireland's oldest and most famous fair, the Ould Lammas Fair that has taken place in Ballycastle for 450 years. Alan and I tried *dulse* (a supposedly nutritious seaweed dried on the local roofs and reputedly good for the brain), while Simon and Sarah stuffed *yellow-man* (a sticky toffee made from a secret recipe) into their little faces. We walked Derry's massive walls and fished for mackerel in the harbour and once, on a brilliant July morning, I stood at the end of a rainbow on a cliff top overlooking Galway Bay.

I was young, I was in love, I had my children with me, and the world was once again my oyster.

As we were about to move to County Down – Alan's demob papers had just come through and he'd found a job in the small seaside town of Bangor – our landlord, Albert Delaney, invited us to a farewell party. Doris, who had returned to England temporarily after a disastrous failed marriage with a young Polish valet (Doris had gone the Toy Boy route before the term was even invented), had been spending a few weeks of that glorious sunny summer with us, and although she never got used to seeing her daughter in fairly straitened circumstances and was still suspicious of the Irish in general and of Alan in particular, she was adapting to the changes with surprising ease. And Doris was never a one to refuse a party invitation.

'Why a farewell party? Farewell to what?' she wanted to know.

'Haven't got a clue. Let's go and find out.'

So off we go to the house next door which Albert Delaney had first gutted, and then done up in very fine style. There was Georgian silver, antique needlepoint chairs, an Elizabethan refectory table, Persian rugs, a gold chalice and curtains of cream damask. And lots and lots of Irish whiskey and Guinness.

'He's not short of a bob or two!' mutters Doris darkly.

'Farewell to what? Where are you going?' she asks Albert Delaney as they clink their brimming glasses of Jameson together, her little brown eyes twinkling at the prospect of a good party.

'To prison,' he replies, not batting an eyelid.

I see my mother wrestle with her natural curiosity, but when Albert is not more forthcoming, Doris, rising brilliantly to the occasion, says: 'Well, that's interesting. I believe prisons are a lot better now than they used to be. You should see the prisons in New Guinea . . .' and she was off, leading Albert into dungeons of meths drinkers, wife-beaters, crazed cult members, cannibals and club-wielding murderers. In contrast, Northern Ireland's infamous Maze prison must have seemed quite a haven to Albert.

We spent seven years in Northern Ireland.

I started work at Ulster Television, an independent television station, where I did everything from newsgathering to Easter Bonnets, and from interviewing a talking dog (who barked 'I want one!' not very convincingly) to interviewing astronomer Patrick Moore who was then Chief Astronomer at the Armagh Observatory.

I then joined the BBC World Service and roamed the length and breadth of Ulster reporting on stories that ranged from drug addiction (then in its infancy in Ireland), to adoptions, Orange Day parades, proselytising Protestant parsons and wily Catholic priests. I learned a lot about myself and about all sorts of things Irish. I spent a particularly memorable day in Bushmills where I learnt that Irish whiskey, unlike its Scotch counterpart, is spelt with an e, and was invented by Irish monks who called it *uisce beatha*, meaning 'water of life'. Legend has it that Queen Elizabeth I once claimed that it was her only true Irish friend.

I moved to BBC Television, where I presented my own talk shows (after going through the paces of a reporter, writer and presenter). The first was called *Late With Kate,* a current affairs show which came on after the Epitaph, so late that not even members of my own family bothered to sit up and watch it.

Then I was given a prime time television talk show at 8 o'clock on a Saturday night called *Kate at Eight*. This show toured the north and south of Ireland and visited England as well. There was a one-page script for a fifty-minute live show. At the top of the page it read 'Roll opening captions', then followed a list of the illustrious guests who might range from Elizabeth Taylor and Richard Burton, Anthony Hopkins and Jackie Stewart, to the Beatles, Clement Freud and Herman and the Hermits. At the bottom of the page it read 'Roll closing credits'. It was a potential nightmare. I had no training, a director who cared more about the angle of his shots and how things looked than what was actually said, and a £60 dress allowance.

Looking back I don't know how I carried it off. But I did. And it taught me once again to be self-reliant and that it's not always (or indeed often) that it's the rich and famous who are the nicest or most interesting people on earth.

And how's this for interconnectedness? One night in the late-Sixties, I was a guest on Gay Byrne's long-running TV show in Dublin. In the green room before, and again on set, I sat next to a black lady singer. I'd never heard of her, but instinctively warmed to her. On the show she sang a song I'd never heard of either called 'The Click Song'. It was Miriam Makeba. I barely knew where South Africa was, or what was going on there, and gave the experience hardly another thought.

Two years later, with a third child, a baby daughter called Tara, Alan and I, Simon and Sarah were on our way to start a new life in South Africa. Today, as I write, I'm working on a script that showcases a famous singer called Miriam Makeba.

And so I came back to Africa. For good. Whilst living in Ireland I had revisited Nigeria and Ghana on several occasions, because before I left Nigeria I had been trained by the Cambridge Examinations Syndicate to be an examiner for the West African

Examinations Board that was then set up for the first time. I had co-authored an English grammar textbook for English-speaking West Africa and subsequently became chief examiner and co-moderator for O Level English Language to the West African Examinations Board. Once a year, for several years, I travelled from Bangor in Country Down to West Africa, once again to immerse myself in the sights, smells and sounds of Africa – the bright turbans of the market women and the flamboyant colours of the exotic trees and flowers; the sweet smell of the earth after rain; rotting dead dogs beside the roads (it was considered very lucky, 'good juju', to run over a dog); the din of constant horn-blowing traffic. I loved the mammy wagons with their unique painted signs. One literary-minded owner-driver had painted the slogan 'The Pen is Mightier than the Sword' on the side of his canvas-covered lorry. But he ran out of space and the side of his passenger-packed mammy wagon proudly proclaimed 'The Penis Mightier than the Sword'.

But as I found out when I went back to Peru, you cannot recreate the past. On these examining trips, I visited Lagos, Enugu (where Sarah was born) and the university town of Ibadan, as well as Accra and Kumasi in Ghana, but I never made it back to Itu and Calabar.

Over thirty years later I spend some time with the Abbot of a Buddhist monastery in the far north of Thailand. He tells me, as he is teaching me Mindfulness, that one must always remember the past and learn from it, but that one should live in the present. Make the most of *this* moment.

Shortly before my visit to the Abbot, I had fulfilled a lifetime's ambition: I visited one of the world's greatest sacred sites – Angkor Wat in Cambodia. This complex of temples based on

Indian cosmology, the cult of Hindu deities and Buddhism – now only the sacred skeleton of a once spectacular administrative and religious centre – sprawls over an area of 400 square kilometres and may well be the most spectacular architectural ruins found on earth.

We arrive in the early morning and gaze across the mist-shrouded encircling moat (representing the oceans) to the thick walls of a huge temple (the walls represent the earth) often described as the Eighth Wonder of the World. Angkor Wat faces west, the place of death in Hindu cosmology, and its five towers – classic temple mountains – symbolise the peaks of the sacred Mount Meru, the Himalayan home of the Hindu gods.

Jayavarman II started the building of Angkor Wat in the ninth century and the complex grew over the next four hundred years until, in the twelfth century, its 100-metre-wide moat which extended over 12 kilometres protected a population of more than a million people. Angkor Wat is the biggest temple of all. Covering an area of two square kilometres with a volume of stone equalling that of the great pyramid of Giza, with its five towers, its perfect symmetry and exquisite bas-reliefs it's one of the most inspired religious monuments ever built – an unrivalled legacy of the once powerful Khmer race. I'm surrounded by beauty, symmetry and mystery.

The statistics are formidable. Six thousand sculptors, forty thousand elephants, and thirty-seven years to build. Thirty-seven hairstyles on the *apsara* (the celestial dancers) representing the thirty-seven levels of heaven. We marvel at thousands of bas-reliefs of Hindu legends that line the walls of the long, first floor stone galleries (the longest in the world) as mynahs strut on the green grass outside and thunder rumbles. This green, green grass throws the thousands of dark grey figures on the walls into striking relief. Interestingly, all are clothed – there is not one naked figure.

As hundreds of sharp-winged swifts wheel around the ancient towers we clamber up a very steep, very narrow stairway to Paradise. There's a chain to hang on to when the steps become even narrower and steeper. A passing monk who squeezes past us tells us solemnly that the way to Paradise is always hard. At the top a statue of Buddha bedecked in strips of gauzy orange cloth greets us. A little old lady, seemingly as old as the temples themselves, sits over an incense burner murmuring soft incantations. I light two sticks of incense as a mark of respect and watch the wisps of smoke curl round the face of the smiling Buddha. Far below, in the dim courtyard, more saffron-robed monks potter about their monkly business. There's a sublime sense of peace.

At Angkor Thom, another temple, a 45-metre tower is topped by four huge carved heads, and surrounded by fifty-four more towers of different levels. But they all have one thing in common – from each a huge, mysteriously smiling stone head gazes down at you. Observers have remarked that the stone faces smile with the cynicism of the ages – they have seen all, experienced all and understand the futility of life. I, however, find the atmosphere intimate and benevolent. As tiny yellow butterflies flit about the huge heads I feel that their smiles are full of peace and quiet fulfilment.

But the jungle lies in wait, crouching patiently round the perimeter of the complex. Beyond the Bayon Temple is that of Ta Phrom, overgrown by jungle and dreamily mysterious, reminding you of what Angkor Wat must have looked like before its restoration when French archaeologists first discovered it lying like a sleeping giant in the primeval jungle.

Here the temple has been left untouched and unrestored. Here the trees and the jungle rule. Giant roots invade walls, seeming to march triumphant over and through once mighty buildings. Huge, toppled heads and remnants of once grand and great statues lie fallen amidst cracked and uprooted paving stones. Tree trunks strangle walls as red and green parrots chatter in the ever-encroaching jungle. Bright green plants sprout and shoot up between overturned carved stone blocks. I clamber through crazily tilted stone doorways, down jumbled steps and along narrow twisted passages. Although it's a mystical, magical, once sacred place, I imagine Indiana Jones swashbuckling his way through here.

'The movie *Indiana Jones* was made here,' says our guide Kim, reading my mind.

As we drive back to the little town of Siem Reap, the jumping-off point for visiting Angkor Wat, Kim tells us that many Cambodians raise crocodiles in their backyards.

'You buy a baby crocodile from one of the lake villages, build a cement pen for it, feed it dead fish once a week, and then after seven years you can get US$ 1500 for it. That's a fortune in Cambodia.'

Kim himself does not raise a crocodile because he was born in the Year of the Dog – and crocodiles eat dogs. It would be the height of cosmic folly for him to raise such a creature as his best loved ones could die as a result. Had he been born in the Year of the Tiger, however, there would have been no problem. Tigers eat crocs.

We take a boat ride – pushing ourselves off sandbanks that rise up through the muddy water – through the floating villages of Tonie Sap, Asia's largest lake. We chug past all sizes and shapes of floating houses, some thatched with palm fronds, some with roofs of corrugated iron. On many decks shrimps are laid out to dry in the sun. Children paddle in large plastic washing bowls from one house to another. A floating shop plies between houses festooned with washing, babies swing in hammocks, women are cooking or tending their 'gardens' – boxes of herbs and flowers attached to the sides of their floating homes. The interiors are spotless, with well-designated areas for cooking, sleeping, socialising and working. Whole families live on a boat that can vary in size from not much bigger than a rowing boat to a small yacht. One smart boat has a TV aerial. There's an atmosphere of total serenity and peace. Birds call, boat engines sputter, women's voices are laughing, hammers knock out new homes, and stretching to every point of the horizon there is open, flat water that melts seamlessly into the sky. Fish jump. In a cage on top of the roof of one floating house, a large, pink fat pig dozes contentedly.

Although there are six villages of about nine thousand people on the lake, mostly Vietnamese, we saw no acrimony anywhere, heard no voices raised in anger, saw no signs of stress, not even a scowl. It must be the Buddhist way, I think to myself, this calm acceptance of what life brings.

It's also impossible, contemplating Angkor Wat, not to consider the transience of life and things mortal. Empires decay, time marches on, the cycle of life is at once exhilarating and relentless. *Carpe diem*. Seize the day. You will walk this way but once.

From Cambodia I went to Vietnam. Who would have thought (those of us who were around in the Sixties anyway) that Vietnam would become a delightful, attractive and fascinating destination? Before I went, indelibly imprinted on my mind were the stereotypical images of napalmed jungle, dirt-streaked GIs, helicopters hovering menacingly over Vietnamese villages and Vietnamese civilians running from bombs. *Apocalypse Now* stuff.

I have vivid memories of a five-year-old Simon running down the path at Ballymaconnell Road in Bangor, County Down, with toy gun in hand, shouting out to sister Sarah, 'Look out! Here I come! I'm a Vietcong guerrilla!'

But that's a Vietnam of the past.

As our gentle Vietnamese guide told me, 'We try to leave the past behind and live for today.'

My journey started in Saigon – now officially called Ho Chi Minh City – but the locals still call it by its former name. The city is a mix of French Colonial and Southeast Asian. The French legacy lingers in sidewalk cafés and roadside vendors offering freshly baked baguettes and steaming cups of aromatic coffee, and in the city's beautiful old colonial buildings, whilst the hustle, bustle and teeming people characterise Southeast Asia. There's a palpable vibrancy, a bustle, a glamour, a frenetic buzz that assails the senses and gathers you in.

The Vietnamese women are among the most beautiful in the world. Outdoors they wear protective face-masks, wide straw hats and elbow length gloves to preserve their pale ivory-coloured skin. They ride past you on their bicycles, scooters and motorcycles – dignified, ladylike and confident in long, sorbet-coloured silken dresses or brightly coloured silk pyjamas, long black shining hair cascading down their slender, straight backs.

I visit the Cu Cui tunnels just outside Saigon with a small group of fellow travellers. These tunnels comprise the infamous 124-mile-long underground network used by the Vietcong during the American War, as the Vietnam War is called by the Vietnamese. The day we visit (we are the only people as it was during the height of the SARS media frenzy) it is pouring with rain and we begin to understand the horrors experienced by both sides alike. Relentless soft rain that wears resistance down and seeps away the spirit. Thick mud underfoot, squelching puddles, dripping foliage.

We bend over almost double and squeeze through tiny openings to go down into the tunnels. Underground, three levels deep into the earth, are handmade weapon factories, casualty posts, meeting rooms, kitchens. Sometimes the soldiers had to lie face down on the tunnel floor in order to get enough oxygen, even though there are concealed airholes every 50 metres. Absolute silence was the order of the day as to be heard was death. We see the handmade Vietcong defences, far from hi-tech but deadly and dreadful. Booby traps, pits full of barbs filed to a gut-piercing sharpness, spikes that leap out of the ground and grab your legs, pierce your lungs or puncture your whole body. Kick open a door and a wall of spikes swings out at you.

In the City War Museum there's an exhibition of famous war photographs by Western photo-journalists – images to haunt the soul. GIs in mud, GIs crying after a failed helicopter raid where most of the crew and passengers were killed, bandaged men tending to wounded comrades, grinning GIs proudly holding up the severed heads of Vietcong soldiers, young men fighting an unknown war, a savage and silent enemy. And always an ever-present fear gnawing at your mind and soul coupled with the terrifying moral issue: Is this a just war? What am I really fighting for?

But then it's back to a gentler and more romantic past. We fly up to Hue, the ancient capital of Vietnam during the Nguyen Dynasty, and visit the Forbidden Imperial Purple Palace, now a UNESCO Cultural World Heritage site, modelled on Beijing's Forbidden City. Even though it was one of Vietnam's most heavily bombed sites, it's still possible to imagine life as it was when the royal family lived inside the walls and the Palace of Supreme Harmony once housed the Emperor's throne.

Cool, quiet pools covered with pale pink lotus flowers are artfully placed throughout the garden of the Forbidden City. Every morning, the tall, globe-like flowers with their enveloping petals open and arch gracefully above their flat, wide, green water lily leaves, symbolising beauty, harmony and peace. At night they furl their smooth petals and wait for the new day. Although the lotus flower is undoubtedly one of the world's most beautiful flowers, it is one of its most functional too. The leaves are used for soup and the wrapping of sticky rice – a favourite Vietnamese food. Its petals are also used for soup, its seeds for insomnia and its flower is pure beauty in a vase. All the parts make up the whole and no Vietnamese home or temple would be complete without its attendant lotus flowers.

A morning dragon boat ride on the Perfume River offers scenes like those of old engravings or silk paintings – a solitary fishing skiff, prow raised out of the water with a woman in a conical straw hat paddling slowly and skilfully against a silver sky and copper-coloured river. We drift towards a famous and lovely pagoda that towers up through the early morning mist and watch old ladies with shaven heads preparing food for the resident monks' midday meal – their only meal of the day. It was from this monastery that the first monk to immolate himself in protest at the horrors of the post-war South Vietnamese government drove all the way to Saigon in a battered old blue motor car. The image of his flaming body went round the world.

We drive over the Hai Van Pass (Pass of the Ocean Clouds) with its spectacular views of forest, mountains and sea on our way to Hoi An, in Vietnam's centre. We lunch at Lotac Beach where we enjoy a sumptuous, freshly cooked meal of fried squid, steamed crab, clams, shrimps and oysters, followed by an instant, fully clothed massage on the beach from beach ladies wearing long, coarse-textured gloves. Hoi An, another UNESCO Cultural World Heritage site, is lovely – a six-hundred-year-old little town which was once an important international trading port. We walk through the jam-packed local market with its tempting, technicolour displays of fresh food and produce and then take a rickshaw ride along a river bank lined with quaint old Chinese houses and assembly halls. There's an old Japanese bridge and shops with cactus plants over the doorways to keep away evil spirits. We feel cocooned in a time warp as we soak up the atmosphere of this charming little town that was somehow bypassed in the wars and conflicts that have assailed so much of Vietnam over the centuries. At the back of the dressmaker's shop where I am being measured up for silk suits, is a courtyard full of singing birds in cages whose sweet notes and trilling songs fill the warm evening air. Their songs compete with the Vietnamese Soap blaring out from a corner TV.

Up north, in Ha Long Bay (yet another UNESCO site) we sail in an old traditional junk through clear emerald waters punctuated with exquisitely beautiful tiny islands, mysterious rock grottoes, caves and small beaches. A dark brown heron flies low over the still water past a bronze butterfly. It's like sailing through a fairy tale.

Hanoi is our last stop – the official capital of Vietnam. I had pictured cold, bleak communist buildings, sterile ambience, a stern, austere bastion of Vietnamese communism, but I was quite wrong.

Hanoi is a charming city that seeps into your consciousness and heart, perhaps my favourite in all of Southeast Asia. I loved this city with its gracious French colonial buidings, its tree-lined streets, its lakes and rivers and its ancient monuments. The Temple of Literature, Vietnam's first university founded in 1070, was built to honour scholars and literary men, and it's impossible not to be moved by its eighty-two imposing stone tortoise stelae on which the names of the 1306 successful examination candidates between 1484 and 1780 are inscribed, evoking memories of those scholarly men who laboured to gain knowledge and recognition all those hundreds of years ago and whose memory is still honoured.

Hundreds of excited schoolchildren in their pioneer uni-forms of short trousers, blouses, peaked caps and jaunty little neck scarves cram into the gardens of Ho Chi Minh's mauso-leum, where against his wishes (he wanted to be cremated) the gentle, wispy-bearded Ho Chi Minh lies in embalmed state. I am told that Ho Chi Minh is not the monster sold to us by the Western media but a mild, progressive visionary, who is to the Vietnamese what Madiba is to South Africans.

I take one of the most exhilarating rides of my life – a cyclo ride (a man-powered, one-person taxi) – through Hanoi's Old Quarter along winding streets whose names have remained unchanged for centuries – Coffin Street, Silk Street, Chicken Street, Toy Street and Basket Street.

Sitting in the back of a cyclo, in the middle of traffic chaos, with bikes, motorbikes, cars, taxis and buses coming at you from every possible angle, is surprisingly calming. It's like being in the eye of the storm.

It's half past five in the evening and the whole of Hanoi seems to be on show – a celebration of life.

Families sit on every spare piece of pavement, usually their own little patch in front of their tiny shop or café. Grannies, babies, dogs. Trees grow in pots and on balconies. Bare-chested men lovingly clean and polish their motorbikes – Hanoi's most prized possessions. People sit at street corner cafés eating and drinking. Old men cool themselves with fans made of palm leaves, or sit hunkered down watching their world go by. Fluffy dogs ride pillion with their motorcycle owners, back legs on saddle, front legs confidently placed on handlebars.

There are trotting women, shoulders bowed under panniers of oranges or litchis, people strolling, women on bikes with their children perched on the handlebars. Horns and hooters blare incessantly. My cyclo driver pedals past an old lady in black pyjamas sitting cross-legged on a small stool. People are drinking out of glasses or small, delicate cups. It seems that the Western habit of slurping from a bottle has not yet reached Hanoi. Cyclo drivers with no fares sit back in the passenger seat of their vehicles and doze amid the din.

I see every kind of pyjama suit from delicate pink lace to blue silk. Most of the erect and dignified lady cyclists and pedestrians wear the ubiquitous conical straw hats and long gloves. Pedalling purposefully, one old lady with pot plants on the back of her bike overtakes my cyclo. Now there are more old ladies cooking over tiny stoves. Young girls strolling arm-in-arm. Another lady with bare feet up on a plastic bucket fanning herself with a painted paper fan.

Vegetables are being prepared, and baguettes, rolls and fruit are for sale all along the pavements. In one narrow street, red and orange silk lanterns turn softly in the evening breeze, along with fluorescent green and purple bird kites. Shops offer teddy bears and toy tigers for sale and a chicken in a straw cage is carried past slung casually on a shoulder. The narrow doorways are crammed with goods. Plastic piggy banks rub shoulders with smiling, flashing, plastic Buddhas. Men immersed in the evening newspaper sit on small stools oblivious to the din.

In Spice Street my senses are dizzied and cloyed by the smells of hundreds of different spices. In Tin Street, welders chink and solder amid clouds of flying sparks. A puppy chained to a tree sits amid a firework display of sparks. I'm pedalled down Toy Street, Food Street, Shoe Street and Silk Street. As we weave through this tumult of life and traffic the cyclo's brakes squeal and grate alarmingly. But although it is the motorbike that rules the streets of Hanoi, it is the family life that dominates the pavements. Life must have been much like this inside the walls of Angkor Wat, where at one time a million people lived. Only walls and ruins remain, but those people of long ago survive in today's people. Perhaps, as Alan has often suggested to me, it is only in generation that we find true immortality.

At dawn the next day I walk to the city's central lake, Hoan Kiem Lake, which takes its name from a fifteenth-century legend about a magic turtle that lent a sacred sword to the young nobleman who led his people to victory over the invading Ming army. It's said that on still mornings when the temple bells sound and the mist is rising from the waters of the lake, a huge turtle can sometimes be seen lifting its great head above the surface. Cynics say that the government puts one there every now and again to keep the legend going.

I see no turtle (although at a dazzling display of Hanoi's unique Water Puppets, a golden turtle figures prominently) but watch thousands of people – old and young – doing their morning exercises. I photograph a very old man meditating beside the lake as wisps of morning mist trail over the water. I am gently welcomed to a t'ai chi class. Although there are so many people, each individual seems cocooned and serene in his or her own activity – secure and confident in their own private space.

A couple of months later I am with the Buddhist Abbot in his monastery outside Chiang Mai in the north of Thailand. He has graciously allowed me time to study Mindfulness with him. We talk first about Buddhism.

'In other religions – although Buddhism is not a religion but a way of life –' he hastens to assure me, 'it is often the supernatural that is the focus. But Buddhism is about humans. The focus is on a human being learning about himself.'

At the back of the temple classroom a clutch of attendant saffron-robed monks nod their heads in agreement and twitter quietly.

'Reincarnation seeks to get rid of the three major characteristics of a human being – ignorance, attachment and desire. Enlightenment – Nirvana – is the state of freedom we can achieve when we rid ourselves of these characteristics.'

Outside the temple bells swing in the wind, their soft chimes wafting through the palm trees and surrounding forest.

'How does one start to do this?'

'Walk the middle way between the abstract and the material. Choose a way of wisdom rather than a way of violence.'

I point out that that's easier said than done.

His unlined, round, honey-brown face (he could be any-where between twenty-eight and seventy-eight) breaks into a smile.

'Start with loving kindness. Be kind even to the tiniest creatures. For example, rather protect yourself against a mosquito then kill one. Remember, wholesome action produces good deeds and thoughts that in turn produce a good karma. Follow the Buddha, but again remember that the Buddha says, "I can show you the way, but it's *your* choice." '

After two days of discussion and learning meditation techniques, I thank him as I leave the gates of the monastery.

But before I set off down the long brown mud road leading back to the modern world, I turn and ask him, 'Have you ever had any doubts?'

'About what?' he replies, surprised.

'About the Buddhist Way being the One, True Way.'

He thinks for a moment then smiles gently.

'Not at the moment.'

His attendant monks smile and twitter happily.

Before I leave he tells me once again, 'Be concerned with life today. Not with yesterday and tomorrow. That doesn't mean that we forget the past, but that we learn lessons from it, and then move on.'

That's pretty good advice, whether you're a Buddhist or not.

Ibsen's Peer Gynt likens a human being to an onion which, when peeled, layer by layer, skin by skin, is eventually reduced to nothing. It's a very sad and nihilistic view of life. I believe just the opposite. I believe that life is like the lotus flower with its many enfolding petals. I believe that all of life's experiences, from childhood to the end of our days, happy, sad, simple, complicated, beautiful, ugly, fleeting and lasting, enrich our lives, so that from nothing we build up layers of an enfolding wisdom based on experience. We become beautiful and functional – just like the lotus flower.

And every day we have a new beginning . . .

13

Alan's Chapter

'Tis all a Chequer-board of Nights and Days
Where Destiny with Men for Pieces plays
Hither and thither moves, and mates, and slays,
And one by one back in the Closet lays
Rubáiyát of Omar Khayyám

When it was suggested that I write a chapter for *Doing It With Doris* I asked what the book was going to be about.

Alarm bells started to ring in my head when the answer was, 'Well, it's about a journey.'

'A journey? From where? Where to?'

'Not that sort of a journey, a journey through life.'

'Not another "meaning of life" thing, is it?'

This was sounding suspiciously spiritual. Readers of my chapter in Kate's first book, *There's More To Life Than Surface*, may remember that in my chapter 'Dancing to a Different Drum' I made it quite clear that as far as I am concerned there is no meaning to life. If it's a journey, it's a journey from nowhere to nowhere, a collection of random happenstances.

So when I consider my own insignificant part of the greater insignificance, I cannot discern a pattern, or the pattern is that there is no pattern. Some things have made me laugh, some have made me cry. Some are funny, some tragic. Is there a linking thread? I can't find one, unless I choose to find a *subjective* link, which is me, events are related to one another only through my erratic bouncing through life, ricocheting from wall to wall of an unseen destiny.

In my groping for a pattern, I can dimly perceive that the absence of a pattern is pattern enough. That the string of unconnected episodes of my 'journey' could be said to conform to some sort of overall 'meaning'. It may be that the death of a sparrow or the fall of a leaf both have their place in some sort of natural progression? Let alone the fall of an emperor or the death of a pop star? Beats me.

There is no overall reason, there is only a subjective comfort and joy in family and friends. That's what it's all about. And that's all that life itself is, and if anyone can trace out a theme for the disjointed and arbitrary meanderings of his destiny, then good luck to him. We're born, we live, we die, and if we're lucky we find and give some happiness along the way. So the rambling stream of my life sometimes lifts memories to the surface, whirls and eddies, slows in calm backwaters, struggles over rocky patches, and carries on to . . . where?

The only connecting theme to remembered people, communities, events, emotions is . . . me. But life is fun, isn't it?

Enough preamble. At the age of eighteen I was working on a farm up in the western Highlands in Scotland. Your Highlander is not the welcoming big-hearted giant that he's popularly supposed to be. He is in fact hostile, reserved and suspicious of all strangers. When he gets to know you, then it is a different matter, then he is the salt of the earth, but he doesn't give his trust lightly.

The Great Glen Cattle Ranch stretches for six miles along the road that runs north from Fortwilliam to Inverness, directly under the brow of Ben Nevis. Ben Nevis may be the highest mountain in the British Isles but I was chagrined when I staggered to its lofty peak to encounter two elderly (*really elderly*) ladies who had strolled up an easier route. That was a warm and sunny day, but a few days later, on the first of September, when the annual race up Ben Nevis was taking place, we farm workers were called out from the local Saturday night dance to comb the heather for a climber who had strayed off the track. The Highlands can be benign one minute, fierce and merciless the next. That young climber was alive when we found him but dead when we got him down.

Every year the circus came to Inverness, and apparently every year the workers on the Great Glen Cattle Ranch had determined to go the circus, but every year something had prevented it. This year we had really planned it. Keenest of all was old McKay, our foreman, or gaffer. He was a little wisp of a man, looked as if a mild breeze would topple him, but he was as tough as old boots and would labour on in the fields when we youngsters were near collapse. He was from the islands, spoke scarcely a word of English, so had to swear at us in Gaelic when we displeased him, and he was intensely patriotic. When he heard the Queen and Prince Philip were visiting Scotland his patriotic fervour knew no bounds. All the farm hands, twenty of us, were put to work driving all the cattle up and over a mountain so that we could line them up on the side of the road and demonstrate the spirit of the Great Glen. Someone suggested it was a cattle ranch so we should ride horses for the round-up. But that plan was abandoned when one man fell off and broke a leg, and another broke an arm. Eventually, on a beautiful Sunday morning, we had all seven hundred head of cattle lined up beside the fence on the main – and only – road to Inverness. And all of us in our best bibs and tuckers standing respectfully by. The royal couple were late. We stood patiently for hours. Old McKay went behind a haystack to relieve himself, and whoosh! a big black car with Queen and consort flashed by. We didn't like to tell old McKay, and at first he didn't believe us. His disappointment after the weeks of anticipation must have been intense. But when he finally accepted the truth, he didn't say a word about it, just got us driving seven hundred head of cattle back over the mountain.

Anyway, this year we were ready for the circus. The menfolk only, because it was much too important an occasion to include wives and bairns. Many of the men worked their own little crofts as tenants on the ranch, and we set out very early in the morning in an old purple ex-Canadian airforce bus, to drive the 60 miles to Inverness. We stopped at the crofts along the way. Wives and children came out to wave their menfolk off, giving them little parcels of food for the journey. It was six miles through wonderful highland heather to a crossroads known as Spean Bridge. There was a pub at Spean Bridge into which we trooped – all twenty of us – and although it was still pre-dawn the bar was soon doing a roaring trade. Near midnight we helped each other out of that bar, drove the six miles back to our ranch, stopping frequently to urinate and or throw up in a ditch, and arrived home to tell the wives and bairns that once more we'd missed the circus.

The full moon gazed dispassionately down on Ben Nevis, the white ribbon of road winding northwards from Fortwilliam, and the poor benighted souls who were perhaps vaguely aware that this day had not passed as planned. Blind mouths we were.

Perhaps when I look back on life, and I recollect certain locations and events, I have a glimmer of a perception of compassion for mankind. Compassion and respect too. We may not know where we're going, most of us, or discern a path, but we keep on going. Like insects driven by instinct to ceaseless effort.

Whenever two ex-servicemen get together, they naturally reminisce about their experiences. Bertie, my elder brother, pointed out once when we were doing precisely that, that it's funny how we always remember the good times, the humorous things, and we forget our less-than-amusing adventures. It's true and right now I'm remembering one particular incident.

In 1960 I was seconded from the British Army, from the Royal Irish Fusiliers, to the Nigerian Army. The Fusiliers were shortly afterwards involved in one of those regimental amalgamations that always offend and disgust all personnel affected, and there was in fact an amusing side to that. There were three regiments in the North Irish Brigade up until they all became part of the newly formed North Irish Rangers. The three regiments included the Royal Irish Fusiliers, whose regimental emblem was an eagle, dating back to the capture of a standard from the French during the Peninsular War. The emblem of the second regiment, the Royal Ulster Rifles, was a harp and so a miniature harp adorned their headgear and their epaulettes. And the emblem of the third regiment, the Royal Inniskilling Fusiliers, was a fuse, a component that enables a grenade or bomb to detonate.

Well, when the traditions of a regiment are threatened, the resulting uproar is greater by far than any battle in the past. It's understandable too, because regimental colours and honours won in long-past campaigns in far-off places form part of that cement that binds servicemen in generation after generation, an essential component of that *esprit de corps* that is indispensable to the fighting capability of any unit. Opinions and suggestions as to a new emblem flooded in, to military authorities, to newspapers, to regimental magazines, to the War Office. And not just in Ireland, it was a national crisis, of a greater magnitude than any famine or national disaster. And not just in Ireland, because similar amalgamations were being implemented throughout the whole British Army. The point of all this background is to explain the climate in which a retired army colonel wrote to the press with an excellent suggestion. Each of the three regiments had a valid reason for promoting its own claim to a continuum of its history, so the only fair thing to do was to create an amalgam of all three regimental emblems. His suggestion was an eagle playing a harp with a fuse stuffed up its arse.

The thing is, there is often a schism between the proud and noble traditions of the military and the day-to-day conduct of the warriors. Don't get me wrong, I loved army life. But that didn't blind me to some of the farce which was interwoven into the army structure, some farcical events which we remember almost with affection, because we forget the emotions of annoyance and frustration that prevailed at the time.

I'm thinking of one particular army exercise in Nigeria in 1962. The army loves 'exercises', and they are invariably magnificent opportunities for what can go wrong, regardless of planning and rehearsals. Our battalion, 1st Battalion of the

Queen's Own Nigeria Regiment, was stationed at Enugu, the capital of Nigeria's then Eastern Region. Our combined army and police exercise had been planned with the objective of catching smugglers who were allegedly bringing vast quantities of contraband into Nigeria from the Cameroons and from Fernando Póo, an island off Nigeria's western coast. I was a company commander and my company was assigned certain towns and villages to secure.

My infantry company consisted of three platoons, with three NCO platoon commanders, and a company headquarters, and numbered about a hundred bodies in all. The soldiers were mainly of the Hausa tribe, from northern Nigeria. At that time they were mostly uneducated and illiterate, but excellent and reliable infantrymen. The first town we were supposed to secure was a fairly large centre of a rural area. The jungle grew up to the edges of the town, equatorial vegetation. I posted a sergeant with one platoon at the town centre, where five roads converged. His instructions were to stop and search road traffic for contraband. I left that platoon and set off with a driver in a Land Rover to visit another platoon that was positioned an hour's drive away. Returning to the first town in the dark, we came around a corner to be confronted by a tree trunk across the road. No sound, no sign of people. We got out of the vehicle and lugged the tree trunk into the bush and continued on our way.

Back at the town, we found the night alive with music, soldiers, civilians, police. Scattered lights provided some illumination. Our arrival at this Dante-esque scene coincided with the arrival of a municipal employee on a bicycle. These employees were known as native messengers, and wore a semi-military uniform. He had no lights on his bicycle, was smoking a cigarette, recognised me as an officer, threw up a smart salute (cigarette still in mouth) and rode into a thick coil of concertina barbed wire. As he was being extricated from the barbed wire, his uniform in tatters, I asked the platoon sergeant to report on anything that had happened in my absence. The only thing worth reporting was that a prosperous local citizen, driving a Mercedes with no lights, had also driven into the wire. All four tyres were punctured and wire was wrapped around the axle. When I asked what had been done for the driver I was told that he was given a ticket by the police because his licence was out of date, cautioned for driving without adequate lighting, and sent packing. The police were very zealous because they were being backed up by military might and were making the most of it.

By this time the whole town was in festival mood, lots of singing and shouting, popular music blaring from speakers. I decided that my presence wasn't helping so I went back to my Land Rover and driver. A crowd of civilians pressed around us. They were in high good spirits. The monotony of rural life was not often enlivened by anything so exciting as a visit from soldiers and police. I told the driver to start the engine but as soon as he did so the noise from the crowd of spectators rose to an unprecedented pitch. It appeared there was a man under the vehicle!

'Well, tell him to get out,' I instructed the driver to convey in the vernacular.

After some discussion the driver told me that the man couldn't get out from under the vehicle.

'Why can't he?' I asked.

By this time it must have been about one o'clock in the morning and I was beginning to become very exasperated. After another conference with the crowd, the driver explained that the man had no legs. He added that the cripple was asking for money.

'What does he want money for?'

More discussion, while drums beat and someone in the crowd produced some fireworks that added to the symphony of barking dogs, drunken laughter and random screams.

'He wants money for the cinema, sah!'

More delighted laughter from the crowd.

It was explained to the crowd that I was about to drive off and the cripple's predicament wasn't my highest priority. Whereupon a man with no legs pulled himself out from underneath my vehicle on a small wheeled trolley. I wanted to ask what film was showing at the cinema at this impossibly late hour, and if indeed there was electricity available, but I think I realised that I was on the verge of hysteria myself, or perhaps insanity, and that there was a real danger of me joining in the festivities, drinking the beer that was offered by the crowd and of singing and shouting along with the rest.

We left the scene of Rabelaisian excess and returned along the road to revisit the outlying platoon. It was by now about three o'clock in the morning and the tree trunk was back in place. This time there was a crowd of noisy drunken peasants armed with a collection of home-made small bore muskets and even a blunderbuss or two and they made their demands known to the driver. It appeared that they had declared a state of unilateral independence for their village, and we were required to pay a toll fee that had been introduced that very night. I was armed with a Sten, a sub-machine gun, and I stuck the muzzle out of the window and fired a long burst into the air. In a flash the crowd disappeared and we were left with silence and stillness, stillness except for the leaves that were fluttering down in the moonlight, leaves that had been blown off the over-hanging trees by my burst of fire.

The Nigerians were a cheerful and likeable lot. The previous year our battalion had been in the Congo, part of the United Nations Peace-keeping Force that was supposed to maintain law and order in a maelstrom of rape, murder and treachery. The local population where we were stationed were Balubas, a bloodthirsty group of the most villainous type. In our initial briefing by an English major, we were told – along with a lot of other useless information – that one of the things we shouldn't do was to take photographs of villagers in the region. The local villagers believed that cameras stole their souls, and would understandably react in a hostile manner.

A few days later, on patrol in Kasai Province, I stopped my vehicles at a kind of crossroads where a scattering of tribespeople gazed at us with sullen and dangerous expressions. I produced a camera and as I lifted it a clamour from the Balubas made me pause. When it was explained by our interpreter that I meant them no harm, but just wanted a few photographs, the answer was that I must wait for a short while. Then this crowd of piratical-looking villains disappeared into the jungle – to change their rags of clothing for finery more suitable for a photograph!

Farce and tragedy went hand in hand in the Congo. Unbelievable atrocities and unexpected dignity and kindnesses. Humour and violence. A view of the human condition at once depressing and uplifting. I went to Port Franqui, a town way up on a massive bend in the mighty Congo River where it turns west and heads thousands of miles towards the Atlantic Ocean. Heart of Darkness country. A couple of months previously, a Swedish doctor had lain hidden in the river and breathed through a hollow reed stem while his companions were slaughtered on the river bank.

The night I arrived I visited the town's most prestigious hotel. A broad stairway spiralled gracefully upwards in a spacious ballroom. A magnificent chandelier hung from the lofty ceiling. There were no Belgian hotel managers left, no management of any kind, but unpaid staff kept cleaning and maintaining this imposing relic. Everything sparkled and glittered. Why? It could only have been because the staff was compelled to seek order and meaning in the collapsed infrastructure. Disorientated, not knowing what else to do, they kept on cleaning and polishing and brushing and dusting and putting out silver and damask at place settings that would never be filled. I wouldn't be surprised to learn that they were still doing it today, forty years on, cocooned in a time capsule hurtling towards infinity.

People spend considerable effort in attempting to impose a pattern on life and death, on the 'meaning of life', unable for some inbuilt instinctive reason to accept that there is no pattern, no meaning. But I believe that much of the joy in life derives from the very fact that life and death and everything in between is inexplicable and unpredictable. Whether we're talking individuals, communities or nations, it's the foibles and idiosyncrasies of humans, the inconsistencies and illogicalities of humankind, that accumulate in our memories and our psyches to give to each of us our own individual view of life.

I'm Irish. When people ask me to tell them about Ireland, to describe what's different about it, to explain why Ireland and the Irish have a special place in the world's imagination, the best I can do is recount the events of a particular day in my youth.

During the Second World War, Northern Ireland was subject to the same restrictions as the rest of the United Kingdom. Rationing was enforced, particularly food rationing. Southern Ireland, Eire, was neutral during the war so rationing was not enforced. As there is only a land border between Northern and Southern Ireland there existed an excellent climate for a thriving black market, up until rationing was lifted in the 1950s.

So on a glorious Spring day in the early Fifties Denis and I, both teenagers, set out in Northern Ireland to do our bit to relieve the famine. We cycled from our homes in County Down, up over the Mountains of Mourne. A wonderful morning, rabbits playing in the mountain meadows. It's 26 miles from our hometown to a place called Warrenpoint, on Carlingford Lough, from where one took a ferry across the Lough. It was an increasingly warm day, an unbelievably hot day in fact, and subsequently we decided that the events which took place on that day were due to the unusual heat of the sun.

We left our bicycles in Warrenpoint and embarked on the ferry which ran between Warrenpoint and O'Meath, a small village across the border in Eire. It's quite a long ferry ride, about thirty minutes. On board the ferry were the ferry master, an elderly pipe-smoking individual, Denis and I, and about one dozen women who were going across on their weekly shopping expedition for butter, cheese, eggs and other luxuries. The ladies murmured quietly among themselves, the sun beat down and sparkled on the water. I realised that I had no idea of precisely what goods we should buy, so I asked Denis.

'Sugar,' he said firmly. 'Nothing but sugar, my mother says.'

We docked in O'Meath and walked up the main and only street. The street was lined with single-storeyed false-fronted stores, just like in an old Western movie. The sun was still fierce.

Denis led the way into the first shop that looked like a grocery. The interior of the shop was narrow and quite dark, stretching right up to the back door of the premises. A middle-aged lady stood behind the counter and enquired if she could help us.

'I'd like some tea, please,' said Denis.

'Certainly, sir. What brand would you be wanting?'

This was where things started to go wrong. Denis had no more knowledge of the different brands of tea than I had, but what he said was, 'What brands do you have?'

It turned out that the lady stocked an amazing variety of brands of tea, which she proceeded to recite. The more brands she mentioned the more confused Denis looked. Warming to her subject, the shopkeeper dragged out a set of stepladders and ascended to higher and higher shelves. We would never have believed how many options we had.

I'm standing behind Denis when I say, 'Hey! I thought you said we should only buy sugar?'

Denis swung round, shock and surprise on his face.

'What! Did I say *tea*?'

He turns back to the woman.

'Sorry, I've changed my mind, do you have any sugar instead?'

The lady is standing near the top of her ladder, an outstretched hand clutching a final offering of tea cartons, the contents of the lower shelves scattered all over the floor.

'You don't want any tea then?'

'No. Sorry. Only sugar.'

She descends the ladder slowly, throwing the last two cartons to join the dozens of others on the floor.

'What would you be wanting, sir?'

'Some sugar, please.'

'Sorry. We're out of stock of sugar, would there be anything else?'

'Er, no, thank you.'

And Denis turns to stand beside me.

'What would you be wanting, sir?' the lady asks me.

'No, it's all right, I only wanted some sugar too.'

'Certainly, sir. How much would you like?'

When I ask for four pounds of sugar she turns away and walks through a door in the rear wall of the shop, emerging after a moment or two with the four pounds of sugar. I thank her, pay her and turn towards the shop's exit. Denis has been watching this little scene. The Irish are a polite nation and usually prefer the indirect to the direct question.

'Can you tell me where *I* can possibly buy some sugar?'

'You could try the butcher's next door.'

We thank her and head for the exit.

The butcher's next door is like a mirror image of the first shop. We approach the counter and when there is no sign of service, Denis knocks loudly. A door at the back opens and *the same woman* enters.

'Good morning, gentlemen. What can I do for you this fine morning?'

As if she has never set eyes on us before this moment.

'I'd like some sugar, please,' says Denis.

'Certainly, sir, how much would you be needing?'

When he asks for four pounds she exits the rear door to return a few moments later with the sugar.

When we leave the shop Denis stamps backwards and forwards with the parcel in one arm, beating his head with his free hand.

'It's the sun, it's the sun,' he repeats.

After all this it's time to catch the ferry back to Warrenpoint, but the delights of the day are not yet fully over. We trudge down the jetty clutching our sugar. On the ferry are the same ferryman and the same ladies returning with their bags full of contraband. But there's an additional passenger on this return trip. A man of perhaps forty years, he is dressed in a full three-piece business suit, waistcoat buttoned, hat on head, briefcase in hand. He would have stood out at any time in this setting, but on a rural Sunday morning he really looked special. We cast off, the women talk quietly to one another, the ferryman sucks on his pipe. The sunlight bounces off the water. The stranger sits in front of me looking straight ahead. Denis and I sit with our own thoughts. The outboard motor chugs on, we slowly approach the Warrenpoint jetty. The ferryman cuts the motor and we drift in.

The only explanation I can give for what happens next is that when you're on a boat and the engines stop and there's silence in place of the engine's noise, you can have a feeling that movement has also stopped. That's what I think, when the businessman in front of me stands up abruptly and steps over the side of the boat into some five feet of sea. He's not about to lose face, not this fellow, he raises the hand holding the briefcase up above his head and strides out for shore. You'd think anyone would say, 'Oh shit! Look what I've done!' Or something similar. But not our man. After one shocked and astonished glance at this unusual development, all the boat's occupants look fixedly ahead, because the Irish are naturally polite and none of us wants to embarrass the gentleman. He on his part behaves as if this is the way he always gets off the boat, and his walking pace through the waves matches the speed of the boat, so that he remains abreast of the remaining passengers.

When we reach the jetty he doesn't even squeeze the water out of his clothes, but strides out, hat still on head, briefcase in hand. I would have loved to have been a fly on the wall in whatever room he was attending a meeting in. I only hope he got whatever contract he was bidding for.

That's Ireland for you.

In 1970 we emigrated from Ireland to South Africa. Today we live in Johannesburg, but my work takes me often to neighbouring territories. One of my favourite destinations is Botswana. It's a desert country and the desert breeds its own characteristics in people. Batswana, as the inhabitants are called, are in the main unsophisticated, polite, straightforward and friendly. It's a harsh country for the most part, and it breeds fortitude in its people.

In 1994 I drove from Johannesburg to Gaborone, the capital of Botswana. I stopped at the Oasis Motel, on the road into the city, to say hello to my friend Richard Spring. Richard ran the Oasis Motel, and he said he was very pleased to see me because he was having a lunch party at the Oasis and he wanted me to meet another friend of his, Charlie Sheldon. Charlie and I had known about one another for years, but had never met. Before we could say anything else, Charlie said he had experienced something strange with his 4x4 vehicle, which was that the rear windscreen wipers could not be turned off.

It sometimes happens that a day dawns and all kind of vibrations tell you that this day is going to be different. I told Charlie that my hire car was parked outside and, believe it or not, *its* windscreen wipers could not be switched off. We trooped outside where the two vehicles were parked side by side and both sets of wipers were in frantic operation. This astonished us and set the tone for the rest of the day. Present at lunch were Peter Sandenberg, owner of a safari camp in the Okavango Delta, two of Charlie's teenage sons, a house-sitter, Richard Spring and myself. Wine and conversation flowed and the prawns were superb. Towards the end of the afternoon we adjourned to Charlie's home to swim in his pool and to continue our revels.

At about ten o'clock I left to drive to my hotel in Gaborone, refusing all offers to stay the night. When I drove out of the gateway, I made only one mistake – I turned right instead of left. It was only one simple mistake but it was a bad one. Mokolodi was already on the edge of the Kalahari desert and within minutes I realised I was on the wrong road. I decided to carry on, on the grounds that the road must be going some-where, a decision possibly influenced by the wine we had been drinking. And that was another mistake.

The road, or track, kept deteriorating. It's a peculiarity of men, I think, not shared by women, that we find it hard in such circumstances to give up and start again. It's like our reluctance to ask directions – we'll drive for hours rather than stop and ask. I rationalise this by explaining that no one you question is able to give a simple answer. They don't speak your language or they have just this very hour arrived in this location to stay with a cousin, or their explanations are too convoluted to help or – not infrequently – they confidently give you directions which if followed will take you miles on a totally wrong course.

And so I continued, but eventually could go no further because my vehicle got stuck in a sand drift. It was now the early hours of the morning, and there was no sign of life anywhere. My only option seemed to be to remain where I was and hope that daylight would arrive with a solution. I was miles out in the wilderness. Alternatively, I could attempt to retrace my path, on foot. This was an opportunity for another bad decision, so I tried to retrace my path.

There was no light, not even moonlight, but the white sand of the track could be discerned, with difficulty. I jogged for a few hundred metres, until I twisted my ankle, after which I hobbled until I lost the track altogether. But I persevered, until I could perceive a very faint light in the distance. I had a new problem when I came up against a tall game fence. Left or right? This happened a few times with arbitrary decisions being made in an increasingly reckless mode. I knew I was somewhere in the vicinity of a lion enclosure, and I got something of a jolt when my outstretched hand touched warm hide. It turned out to be a cow, which was no doubt as surprised as I. On, on, on. Another faint glow emerged in the darkness, slightly to one side of my latest route. I turned towards it. I soon discovered this latest glow was coming from a rondavel. The rondavel was protected by a good thorn boma, which I discovered when I walked into it in the darkness. Twice. I found the opening in the boma and then the entrance to the rondavel. The light was coming from a substantial log fire, and a few blanket-wrapped motionless forms circled the fire. I sat down and leaned against the wall and smoked a cigarette. One figure at last stood upright, approached and sat beside me. Silently I offered him a cigarette, which he accepted in equal silence. After five minutes of silence he asked politely if I came from around here.

'No.'

Thinking perhaps it would be polite to elaborate I said my car was stuck in the sand.

'Where?' he asked.

'Somewhere out there.' I gestured into the darkness.

I asked where I was.

'This is a funeral.'

'Are all these people dead?'

Certainly no other forms had given any signs of life.

'No, only one of them.'

I had set out wearing a white shirt, and now, able to inspect my appearance by firelight, I found the shirt was no longer white. It was entirely red. Bloodstained from my encounters with thorns. My face and arms were scratched and bleeding profusely. I must have been a frightening sight to appear out of the darkness at a funeral gathering.

The ensuing conversation revealed that his name was Joseph, that he had worked in the South African mines for fifteen years and had now returned to retire in his place of birth. Another cigarette, and when I asked him if he knew where Charlie lived I was relieved to learn that it wasn't far away. My new friend Joseph kindly offered to accompany me through the thick bush that we had still to negotiate.

I had a vague idea where the rear door of Charlie's house was. Safely inside, in almost total darkness, there was some confusion when Joseph sat on a couch that happened to be occupied by an Irish wolfhound. When things calmed down and we had found a light switch I located an extra-large flagon of red wine. Joseph and I sat in silence for some time, sipping our wine.

'This is a very good wine,' offered Joseph, as if we were sitting in a gentlemen's club in Johannesburg.

'Yes, it is rather,' I agreed.

A companionable silence lasts until dawn's light signals the new day. Joseph departs promising to return to help me find the car. He and I have only been acquainted for a few hours but

224

we're good friends. I've never seen him since that day but he still exemplifies for me the natural dignity and courtesy of the desert dweller, the philosophical acceptance of anything that life may deliver. We set out after breakfast, myself and Joseph, Peter Sandenberg, the house-sitter and two elderly school-teachers from New Zealand who we co-opted along the way. We found the car and life continued. Possibly with a better understanding of the universality of the human condition when stripped of superficialities.

I've worked at many pursuits and I've often been fired because I suffer from the drawback of not getting along with bosses. Can I help it if I have always worked for stupid bosses? I'd be a total fool to pretend that my path through life has been nothing other than delightful and amusing. I have found that in the simpler, more rustic occupations you tend to get more honest people, more straightforward types. I've seen laziness at all levels, I've seen cowardice amongst supposed leaders, I've seen dis-honesty in many guises, but I must admit that I've encountered more dishonesty, cowardice and deceit in the business world, than anywhere else.

When we arrived in South Africa in 1970, my profession at that time was in computers. I joined a major South African organisation that had an exciting and challenging career to offer.

After two years of challenging work I fell out with my boss and was eventually fired. I really quite enjoyed the experience of being fired because the boss had a bad stutter and I was able to deliver ten insults to every one of his.

But life goes on and eventually I ended up self-employed – which meant my boss was now more impossible than any of his predecessors!

What it all means is, you have got to live life. Take the thick with thin, the rough with the smooth, the laughs with the tears. And understand that there is no precedent for anything. There are, of course, consequences.

About eight hundred and fifty years ago the Persian poet Omar Khayyám wrote:

The Moving Finger writes; and, having writ,
Moves on: nor all thy Piety nor Wit
Shall lure it back to cancel half a Line,
Nor all thy Tears wash out a Word of it.

14

Picnic on a Mine Dump

Over thirty years ago, Alan and I, Simon and Sarah, with a new baby daughter, Tara, arrived from Ireland one cold windy morning in Cape Town. Alan and the baby had been up since dawn as our ship, the SS *Vaal*, sailed into Cape Town harbour. Alan was determined to see Francis Drake's legendary Fairest Cape on all the Earth. The rest of us had succumbed to the notorious Cape Rollers and were lying below, too ill to care where we were.

'How many children?' growled the scowling white South African immigration officer.

'Three.'

'Not enough!' he barked.

You're lucky to have three, I thought, because we'd nearly gone to South America instead. It was a toss up which job for Alan came through first. We were still waiting for Brazil to confirm our passage to Rio when the South African immigration authorities in London asked for a photograph of the new baby. We couldn't find one. So we borrowed one from the neighbours next door. Their baby was roughly the same size as Tara, even though it was a boy and called Dermot O'Hara. Anyway, as Alan pointed out, all the authorities wanted to see was that the baby was white. So Dermot O'Hara became Tara Turkington and an acceptable new immigrant for South Africa. And Johannesburg beat Rio to the chase.

We spent three windswept, cold, rainy days in Cape Town. All we knew of South Africa was that it was supposed to be warm and sunny and there were lots of private swimming pools. As we sat huddled round the one-bar electric fire one night, in the sparse accommodation provided by the immigration authorities, lamenting the Aran jerseys and hot water bottles we had left behind, twelve-year-old Simon, never one for many words, announced grimly: 'I think we've made a terrible mistake.'

We all looked at one another in dire dismay, then saw the funny side of the situation and burst out laughing.

Fortunately the years ahead would prove him wrong.

At the end of the three days we piled into the car with all our worldly possessions and set off for Johannesburg, to Egoli, City of Gold, and into the unknown.

'Drive straight along here to the robot, turn right and then keep going,' a gap-toothed man in a felt hat advised us.

We drove and drove looking for a robot. We wrongly assumed that it was some kind of advertising gimmick and that a large robotic figure would be standing beside the road. Nobody told us that South Africa is the only country in the world where they call traffic lights robots.

However, we eventually found the right road and drove up from Cape Town in our old blue car, the survivor of seven years in Ireland, puttering through the Karoo in springtime, stopping at Laingsburg, where the rooms cost two rand a night and they wouldn't let me into the bar for a drink.

'No women allowed!'

I nearly turned round and went straight back to County Down.

We arrived late one Friday night at the Diamond Horseshoe Motel in Kimberley and asked for rooms. The place was packed with huge red-faced men all of whom seemed drunk and disorderly.

The manager burst out laughing.

'Are you joking? It's the Currie Cup. We've no accommodation at all.'

We'd never heard of the Currie Cup. Let alone that this was the first time it had been played in Kimberley. I uncharacteristically burst into tears.

'I'm in a new country,' I sobbed. 'I've a little baby who is hungry and tired and two other children who are bewildered and disorientated. We've driven all the way up from Cape Town, we don't know where we're going and you've got to find us somewhere to sleep.'

On cue, Tara started to scream and Simon and Sarah burst into sympathetic tears.

Four huge Griqualand West supporters took pity on us.

'Here, Tannie, you can have our rooms.'

The next day we saw our first mine dump. The excitement! We could even see the gold glinting in the dust. We were so excited we ate our picnic at its foot. I still have that photograph.

Tiffany was born three years later at the Florence Nightingale Nursing Home in Johannesburg. The immigration officer would have been proud of me. She was a special child (as all the others were special in their way too) as she was our South African baby, a symbol of our commitment to the new country that would become our permanent home. In the true tradition of our Yorkshire family witches she was born at a blood-red full moon, had a crumpled ear, and gazed about her with eyes of ancient wisdom. Although she was a very big baby (over 4.5 kilograms) she was put into an incubator because during her lightning birth (thirty minutes from start to finish) she had swallowed a lot of fluid. In the neonatal nursery she was surrounded by tiny little hairy premature babies and took such exception to this stereotyping that she screamed so loudly and punched the sides of her glass cage so fiercely that they let her out and put her in a cot beside me. She's been a fighter ever since.

I'm not sure if I believe in angels, but Tiffany certainly seems to have been surrounded by them all her life. She survived a near-fatal rare illness when she was seven – saved by the ubiquitous Doris, who, as I came home from the university where I was a lecturer, was waiting at the front door for me.

Never one to mince words she announced grimly, 'That child is dying.'

Tiffany had been home from school for weeks with some lingering virus that wouldn't go away. Our doctor (whom we later discovered had been struck off the British Medical Register) had continued to prescribe enormous amounts of sulphur drugs that almost killed her.

Doris had arrived from England only two days before and had summed up the situation immediately. Indeed, it was she who recognised the notorious doctor from her daily scanning of the juicier stories in the English daily tabloids. Tiffany was saved, but only just, first by Doris' intuition, and subsequently by a brilliant Johannesburg paediatrician who recognised the rare syndrome immediately and was able to deal with it – he was an 'angel', if you will.

At fifteen, Tiffany had a horrendous horse-riding accident that left her face almost severed in half when she fell over the head of her horse as it took a jump. The horse's shoe caught her face and cut it through to the bone. One eye was hanging out, her teeth were smashed and her nose was broken. Driving like maniacs we got her to a clinic where a surgeon who was in his garden at the time just 'happened' to take the emergency call. He could have been anything from an ENT surgeon to an orthopaedic one – or even a general one. But it turned out he was one of Johannesburg's leading plastic surgeons. Another 'angel', maybe.

I try to keep an open mind about angels because I've talked to so many people who've seen them, been guided by them, and believe in them.

Once, however, a very well-known 'Angel Lady' came out to South Africa from Britain and I was asked to interview her. She kept the radio audience entranced with her tales of Gabriel and Michael, archangels and cherubim, and angels who often come disguised as other beings.

'I've never seen an angel, but I think they may have come into my life now and again,' I told her.

She was overjoyed. Here was a potential initiate, ready to face angels in their glory or in disguise. I was obviously a willing acolyte.

She lowered her thrilling voice to a theatrical whisper.

'All you have to do, my dear, is to look for white feathers. White feathers are angels' calling cards.'

That night when I went out into the garden to feed my dogs, I noticed a clump of white feathers beside the dogs' water bowl.

'Bingo!' I thought.

Then a few metres away I noticed Bowser, my Dobermann, with another clump of white feathers in his mouth. It was a dead dove.

'Bowser! Bad dog!' I shouted in mock horror. 'You've killed the Holy Ghost!'

On another occasion, Tara's car broke down at the side of the notorious Golden Highway beside Soweto. She was on her way to Kimberley. It was a blistering hot afternoon and her old car had no air-conditioning. So she wound the windows down and sat listening to a One Day cricket match between South Africa and Australia while she waited for someone to rescue her. Neither Alan nor I were available for the mercy mission, so we asked Trompie, our motor mechanic and a devout Born Again Christian, if he could go instead.

Trompie told us the story.

'When I got there,' he said, 'there was an angel sitting beside Tara, with one great wing around her shoulders. That's why she had come to no harm.'

But a few weeks later Trompie's credibility was rather dented for me when I asked him if he could service our combi.

'Sorry, not today. I'll be astral travelling.'

I've been 'rescued' in The Outback in Australia's Northern Territory by a very old, very drunk Aborigine. I've also been 'rescued' by a cowboy called Spike (the name was etched into his broad leather belt) on Lookout Pass in The Cascades up near the Canadian border. I was 'rescued' from a nasty looking cottonmouth swimming in the same river as me in East Texas by an African-American TV cameraman called Mike, and once my husband was 'rescued' from the biggest casbah in Morocco by a small cheroot-smoking goatherd. I don't know if any of these rescuers were angels, but I suppose they could have been. And what about the Aborigine guardian of Rita's family, Alfred, who told her to 'go home' to her mother? Was he an angel?

I understand that angels come in many sizes, shapes and colours.

Two years ago, my daughter-in-law Sue was running Comrades for the first time. Comrades is one of the most famous marathons in the world, a race of between 86 and 89 kilometres which is run annually from Pietermaritzburg to Durban in KwaZulu-Natal, or in alternate years the other way round, from Durban to Pietermaritzburg. It's probably the only race in the world where thousands of ordinary people from all walks of life compete against each other for the camaraderie and challenge of being a 'Comrades Runner'. Some people have run the race more than ten times; others, after experiencing the punishing hills and valleys once, swear they will never run it again.

Sue had been training for Comrades for months. Tiny, slim and determined, she set out with other members of her running club, to run the 86.5 kilometres from Durban to Maritzburg. She had pasta-loaded, got her mind and body right, and off she went with the other thirteen thousand hopefuls. She ran really well, she said, but then about only seven kilometres from the finish, 'The wheels came off. I just couldn't go on.'

Out of the blue, a Zulu runner appeared beside her. He was running well, but when he saw her distress, he slowed up, counselled, comforted and encouraged her and got her running again. Then he disappeared into the distance.

Sue finished the race and got her medal, but although she tried hard to find her 'angel', he seemed to have vanished without trace. When she queried the race number she had seen on his chest and back, she was told that no such number had been issued.

When Alan was gravely ill and not expected to live during his long bout with cerebral malaria, the undivided, unstinting, loving care and attention of the Zulu and Xhosa nurses who looked after him in ICU for over three weeks, undoubtedly saved his life. 'Angels' of yet another kind.

During those long awful weeks I would drive to the clinic twice a day never knowing if Alan would be dead or alive when I got there.

One night, when it seemed as if he wasn't going to pull through, I drove home from the clinic hardly able to see because of the tears streaming down my face. As I pulled into the driveway of our thatched house, I saw an owl sitting on top of the garage roof, his wings slightly held out from his body and looking straight at me. It was 'my' owl from Peru, the one I had seen during my ayahuasca-induced vision on my first trip to Peru. The owl that had comforted me amidst psychedelic images of sharp splinters and jagged bursts of unnatural colour and led me into a state of supreme peace and acceptance.

When I got out of my car he didn't fly away but continued to stare at me. His huge yellow eyes transmitted a clear message, and I knew then that my husband was not going to die.

My friend, Denise, a well-known South African magazine editor and travel writer, has a very appealing philosophy as to why she believes in angels.

We're sitting together one night in one of the most remote camps in the world – Kipungani in Kenya, just a few straw huts perched on the beach of the Indian Ocean close to the Somali border. Another strikingly brilliant full moon rides over the silver-streaked sea.

'If by believing in angels, I can make my world a more magical place or transfer the love I believe they give me to other people, then that's good enough for me. To me, angels equal love and without them my world would be a darker, sadder place.'

Many people believe not only in angels, but also in devils. Yes, even the ones with forked tails and pitchforks. When the late Hansie Cronjé, former adored skipper of the South African national cricket team, was alleged to have salted away millions in bribes during his illustrious cricket career, his defence was 'The devil made me do it.' In South Africa, as in other parts of the world, Satanism is practised, but it appears to be more media hype than actual devil worship. But it seems that devils, like angels, can also come in many forms.

South Africa has the highest incidence of child sexual abuse in the world – the figures are almost unbelievable for a country that has achieved so much in terms of human rights and human dignity since its bloodless transition to democracy in 1994. In South Africa, one in three girls and one in five boys (2003 figures from the organisation People Opposing Woman Abuse, POWA) are sexually abused. In some squatter camps – euphemistically known as 'informal settlements' – it is believed the figures are even higher. The current myth that if a man rapes a virgin he will be cured of HIV/AIDS seems impossible to dispel. The eight-year-old daughter of my domestic worker was raped just over a year ago. Her mother cries when she tells me that her lovely little girl is not HIV-positive as a result.

'Thank God for His goodness,' she sobs.

Guild Cottage is one of Johannesburg's oldest homes for

abused children. It was founded in 1907 as a refuge for the widows and orphans of the Anglo-Boer War. Today it offers shelter and a home to eighteen abused children. On a visit there, I meet a forty-something housewife from Sandton – one of Johannesburg's most upmarket suburbs. From the age of five until her late teens, she was repeatedly raped by her father. After many years of living in fear that her secret would be discovered, she finally revealed her past to her husband and children.

All this she told me as we stood chatting at the annual 'thank you' to donors of Guild Cottage. I asked her if she would come on my radio programme and tell her story to listeners. She called me the next day. She had thought long and hard about it and, yes, she would tell her story on radio in order to encourage others to come forward and, by raising awareness, highlight the problem even further. She is a founding member of Adult Survivors of Child Abuse and wants to be known as Sue. She read a poem on air that she had written when she was twelve years old. I was in tears, my technical controller Alfred Hlongwane (himself no stranger to tragedy) was in tears, my producer Nick Ericsson was in tears, and I believe most of the listeners to *Believe It Or Not* were in tears too.

> *Today, I don't want to write a poem, I want to write to you Daddy.*
> *I want to come and talk to you and tell you it's okay.*
> *That somehow inside, I wish I could reach you and go inside*
> *And find out why you turned out the way you did –*
> *Always so angry, always so scary.*
> *Your big body always hurting me.*
> *Your hard, heavy body crushed me so many times.*
> *The pain inside my tummy . . .*
> *Daddy, I am only twelve.*

The thing is daddy, you never told me why?
I never told you that I feel sorry for you.
Who hurt you so badly that you had to hurt me?
Daddy, to be honest, I hate you.
I know one should never say hate, you told me it was worse than
murder.
But daddy, you murdered me and yet I am still alive.
But today I buried myself.
I had a funeral all by myself – no flowers, no prayers, no hymns.
I took each tear that I can remember crying and those I can't
And put them in a box.
Buried them where no one can find them ever again.
From today, I will not feel another thing you do and say to me.
I have killed and buried the essence of me . . .

There will always be times when we have to leave people behind
– as I left Rita and Doris behind – or to bury them metaphorically, as Sue did with her Daddy. Maybe this is when the
angels intervene – to help us. And to show us love.

15

The Ones We Leave Behind

Now I want to tell you about Malcolm's funeral.
We arrived at the farm in Zimbabwe in the middle of a hot, African afternoon. Battered cars and over-laden trucks laboured along the potholed road in the hazy heat. Tall trees blazing with huge scarlet blossoms lined the road from the airport. The road to the farm was lovely – red-brown dirt guarded on both its narrow sides by towering spruces. The five-year drought had broken a couple of months before and now it was impossible to believe the parched earth and dustbowl fields of those few weeks ago. Everything now was lush, verdant and fat – satisfied with life. The tassels of the mealies grew strong and tall and busy small birds flew purposefully from side to side of the track.

We heard the singing before we rounded the last bend to the farm. The farmhouse was white and sprawling – much like other pre-Independence ones. But this one had the look of some medieval castle keep. There were people everywhere, moving or sitting. Chickens scratched about in the way chickens do and sagging lines of not very safe-looking washing festooned the entrance court. Small children with the ubiquitous runny noses of all small children in Africa, peeped from behind their mothers' skirts or continued in unremitting fashion to build their play-play piles of dust and dirt into personal fantasies.

We walked into the house. A smell of wood smoke and pungent bodies everywhere. The overstuffed sitting room with its bright pink velvet furniture and garish wall-hangings of Stags at Bay and Spanish Dancers was crowded with women. As were all the other sitting rooms and small offices and bedrooms and different rooms that seemed to grow organically out of the main part of the house. Ashy faces, stony with grief, pondered us.

I put my arms round the first woman who greeted me.

'Are you Portia?'

'No, I'm Portia.'

She was a woman of perhaps forty plus, whose eyes were swollen with weeping and whose black, shoulder-length, curly wig was a little awry. It felt dry and wiry as I hugged her. There was a faint scented smell like of stage clothes brought out into the light. We both cried quietly for a while as the wig tickled my cheek.

Introductions were made.

'This is Simon, Malcolm's firstborn son.'

Simon, pale and drawn from the shock of his father's death and the hurried flight from Johannesburg, greeted the woman.

'This is Phoebe.'

We'd all heard about Phoebe, Malcolm's adopted Zim-babwean daughter. We had heard of her quickness and cleverness, of her being head of class at the local secondary school and how she would go to Oxford one day, like her 'father'. So this plain, moonfaced, heavy girl was something of a surprise.

'How old are you now, Phoebe?'

'Fifteen.'

She looked ten years older.

An old, old lady, tiny, bent and bowed, was introduced as Portia's mother. She ignored me to clutch Simon's hand and hiss her grief through a few remaining blackened teeth. She then sank down into a little, keening, wizened bundle in a corner where she remained for the rest of that interminable afternoon.

'Do you want to see the grave?'

We followed Portia from the claustrophobic yet welcoming house down to a far corner of the garden. There was a brand new hastily dug flowerbed. Six or eight men were digging deep into the red earth. In the distance across the green fields there were low, green mountains. Cows cropped in the pasture beyond the fence. The men came up out of the pit to pay their respects to the firstborn son. Sarah, firstborn daughter, was acknowledged, but was unimportant in the African Scheme of Things.

A large group of sad-faced schoolgirls, far too pubescent for their black school gymslips, arrived to pay tribute. They had walked a long way.

'There are people here I've never seen,' said Portia. 'Some of them have walked from very far places. They've nothing. Not even shoes. I don't know where they've come from.'

But we learned they'd trekked from the places where Malcolm had been stationed over the past thirty years or so since he had come to Zimbabwe – Rusape and Mount Darwin, Bulawayo and Harare – places where he'd first been a young district officer, later a well-known and much-loved district commissioner, and finally a member of the President's Privy Council.

Portia's two sons from a former marriage, Portman and Robert, came to meet us. They didn't seem to have much substance.

'When Portman came home last night he went berserk,' Portia told us proudly. 'He screamed and carried on and broke things and said what have you done to kill my "father", you wicked woman.'

Portman looked suitably proud.

I looked at Simon, desperately controlling his grief and composure. Perhaps Portman's was the right way.

The long, hot afternoon wore on. Tea arrived about an hour after we were offered it. Although it was officially a 'dry' house, because Portia was a Seventh Day Adventist, a bottle of warm beer was produced for Simon and ceremoniously brought to him on a tray with an embroidered tray cloth, a small smeared glass and a bottle opener.

Articulate, well-spoken women who looked like market women all claimed to me that they were Portia's 'best friend'. I learned later that they were all very important women in this or that government ministry. One was a minister and one was a judge.

Portia took us into the main bedroom to get away from the people so that she could discuss the estate with us. She was an important lawyer.

'Do you know if Malcolm made a will?'

We didn't. The farm, bought shortly after Independence, was now worth millions. She gave Simon his grandmother's wedding ring – such a little ring – and told him to give it to his wife. She explained that Malcolm had wished the estate to be divided among her three children from a previous marriage, and Simon and Sarah. But that surprisingly, 'There is no will.'

Simon and Sarah, shocked and drawn, said that they weren't bothered and all decisions were hers.

We left to go back to the hotel in town. We had declined offers of accommodation from Portia and from well-meaning neighbours. We would meet again about noon tomorrow before the service that was to be held on the farm.

'Do you want to see the body? It's in a funeral parlour in town.'

None of us did. As we left the house and drove again down the long farm road, Sarah shuddered.

'It's all so alien,' she said. 'I can't bear to think of Dad here.'

'But you stayed with him earlier this year.'

'He was here then,' she said simply.

The funeral was a gala occasion. There were several massed choirs, the police band, members of Rotary and the Lions, schoolchildren, students, local farmers, lots of important people from the government and hundreds of unimportant people who had come from far and near because they had admired, respected and loved Malcolm. One old man with bare feet had walked for three days to be there. A posturing, pompous pastor conducted a loud service that an old interpreter then shouted out to the crowds in two different African languages. There was much praising of the Lord and loud hallelujahs. Ululating women added to the din.

I thought how Malcolm, always an agnostic, would have been wryly amused by all this and half expected him to sit up in his large, ornate, polished teak coffin, lift the lid, and say, 'Hold on, chaps! This is all a bit much!'

As the coffin was finally lowered into the red earth, and a solitary bugle played the Last Post, a flock of Abdim's Storks, never seen before or since on the farm, flew down and watched from the edge of the neighbouring field.

The posturing pastor, enjoying every moment of his own endless sermonising, pronounced them 'angels'.

Months later, a box was delivered to my house in Johannesburg. Inside were seventeen plates of various sizes from a dinner service that Malcolm and I had bought in London on our first leave from Nigeria, two years after we were married. And the medals he had earned in Zimbabwe during his other life after he left Nigeria and our seven happy years together.

16

Full Moon at Rocktail Bay

So life is a series of closures too, and our journey together is nearly over. All journeys end with going home, and ours will too.

Walk with me now along a forest path under a green sunshade of intertwined branches and trees. Sunlight slants through the high, filigreed canopy that is alive with birdsong, and leaves and butterflies are in constant motion. Beyond the forest path the low sound of the softly booming surf permeates the murmuring and whispering of the leaves. The forest trail is fragrant with the smell of leaf mould, loam, and dark, rich earth. I can hear the clear, penetrating whistle of a Woodward's Batis, the sharp, staccato croak of a Ross' Lourie and the rising and falling liquid refrain of an elusive Yellowspotted Nicator. A tiny Olive Sunbird peeps over her dainty eggcup nest and a little further on a Puffback Shrike perches serenely on her secure little platform of twigs and moss. A thin twig snake betrays its presence only by the tiniest of rustles as it moves its diamond-shaped head. A breeze drifts through the branches and leaves and adds its notes to the forest melody.

I blink as I emerge from the green darkness on to the blinding whiteness of the sands. Here is one of the world's most beautiful beaches – Rocktail Bay in Maputaland, on South Africa's east coast. It lies on the edge of a coastal forest and in the middle of a protected marine reserve where the narrow coastal strip of forested dunes constitutes some of the highest vegetated dunes in the world. On the other side of these dunes, seven kilometres of desolate and lovely white sandy beaches washed by the gentle surf of the Indian Ocean stretch as far as the eye can see. I snorkel through the rocks and inlets, letting the current move me along. I see halfbeaks, convict fish, a sturgeon, some dory, a giant ray and three octopus lying in wait in their rocky, underwater caves. I feel suspended in time and space.

Later on this evening you and I will sit on this beach under a blazing yellow moon and be connected to the Universe in a way that few people have experienced . . .

If life is a series of beginnings and closures – and we all know the truth of that – there's still some point at which we feel we have to come home. Sometimes 'home' is our childhood home, although often when we try to return we find out that it is not the home we have been longing for, but the childhood. Sometimes 'home' is the place where we have experienced most, loved or suffered most, maybe the family home into which our children are born, grow up and then leave to make their own homes. Sometimes 'home' is a tiny apartment, a room in somebody else's house, or even just a small space behind a curtain in a shack.

But these are real, material homes, built of bricks and mortar, straw and mud.

What about the home of the heart?

The place where your spirit comes to rest?

Where and how do you find those places?

I've been given so many definitions and explanations over the years. I've travelled the world in search of some of them. There are those who believe they will find happiness and ultimate glory in a life to come. Others believe that their spirits return again and again in different bodies, learning the lessons that they failed to learn in this life. Others believe that there are some souls that never find release or salvation but restlessly haunt the corridors of this life, waiting to be admitted to rooms that remain forever closed to them. Yet others find solace in miracles, in major recoveries from terminal illnesses, to the small miracles of kindness and compassion that we witness every day.

Some find soul comfort in meditation, others within the comforting boundaries of an organised religion, yet others in choosing a spiritual path of their own making. Some find a home in Mystical Science, religious fundamentalism, doing good works for others, Eckankar, Pacifism, Non-Violence, Rastafarianism, Evolution, Krishna Consciousness, Quakerism, Neurolinguistic Programming, Neurosemantics, the Superstring Theory, Conservation and Ecology, Liberation Theology, Catholicism, Protestantism, this -ism, that -ism, Aliens, Predestination, Regression Therapy, the Power of Prayer, psychics, faith healers and tarot cards, or their personal relationship with Jesus.

The laundry list is endless.

What life has taught me is that if you want to find your real home – that home where your heart and spirit can truly come to rest – then you must stay open to all people and all ideas. Sometimes you may not like those people or ideas, or maybe you feel threatened by or contemptuous of them. Sometimes you will certainly disagree with them. But it doesn't matter what your reaction is if you respect other people and their opinions, however different from you and your ideas they may seem.

Once, when the poet Samuel Taylor Coleridge was desperately depressed, he wrote about his inability to *feel* anything. He said that when he wrote about the moon and the stars, 'I see, not *feel*, how beautiful they are.'

He is pinpointing the relationship between intellectual awareness and emotional and spiritual awareness.

If you keep your heart and soul options open you will find your true home. Expect that moment of truth and realisation. It may come in strange ways or even mundane ones, but if you keep your heart and spirit open it will come. My moments have come in very dramatic ways. Once in a derelict hut beside the Amazon, once on a beach in Maputaland.

I first found peace and acceptance underneath a blood-red moon in the Amazon, when I experienced a peace that passed all understanding. It's not always with me, I can't always access it, but having once experienced it, I know that it is there in my deepest heart and soul.

The second time those feelings were revealed to me – in a shock of recognition – was under another full moon, this time a blazing yellow one, at Rocktail Bay.

Let's now finish this journey together and go back to Rocktail Bay.

First, let me give you a bit of background.

Sea turtles are one of nature's gentlest creatures and have survived unchanged for over 100 million years, through climate change and asteroid impacts. The Maputaland coastline – from Sodwana Bay to Kosi Bay – is one of the most important breeding grounds along the African coastline for Loggerhead and Leatherback turtles. Every year, between October and February, Loggerhead and Leatherback turtles come ashore at night to lay their eggs in the same area where they were hatched. They are among the most endangered creatures on earth.

It's mid-November, and six of us, (including my friend Gail who was with me in Tibet), and Sylvia of Owl and Pussycat fame, ride in an open Land Rover over the dunes and along the beach.

'It's late in the season,' warns Andy, our guide. 'Our chances of finding a turtle are remote – particularly a Leatherback.'

'You never know what's round the next corner…' I optimistically remember Doris' philosophy.

The iridescent surf booms softly under the blazing full moon. White ghost crabs scuttle across the smooth unmarked sand. Suddenly ahead of us we see the marks of a small tractor heading up towards the high-water mark. But it's not a tractor. The marks are those of a giant Leatherback turtle that has come ashore to lay her eggs.

A turtle lays only every seven years or so, but when she does, she will lay her eggs over a period of a few weeks, wave-hopping until she spies the place on the beach that calls instinctively to her. We plod through the soft sand and follow her marks, and suddenly there she is. I sink to my knees and gasp in awe, wonder and amazement at the huge creature digging in the sand.

Nothing – not photographs, not wildlife documentaries – prepares you for the size of these creatures. She is about two metres long and weighs about 450 kilograms – four of us could sit comfortably on her back. She faces away from the sea as she purposefully prepares her nest in front of us. Her front flippers, huge, twice the size of the back flippers, rest in front of her head (get in the way of one of these and your legs would be snapped like twigs). Their turn to work will come later. It is the back flippers that are doing all the work now, each flipper taking turns to carefully scoop out a deep hole which will eventually be the depth of those flippers. At first, she scoops out great piles of sand. As the hole becomes deeper and deeper, eventually she can only scoop out teaspoonfuls.

At last she is satisfied with her handiwork and prepares to lay. Then the perfectly round, gleaming white eggs, bigger than a golf ball but smaller than a tennis ball, start pulsing out. First one, then another one. Then two or three together, then half a dozen at a time, until she has laid between a hundred and one hundred and twenty eggs. It has taken her many, many years to achieve this moment of fruition, a voyage through time and across the great oceans of the world – a long, solitary journey in the cold black depths of the sea, meeting and mating only once every seven years. As she lays, she is in a deep trance, completely oblivious to our presence.

'You can touch her,' says Andy.

And touch her we do, feeling the icy cold of the deep, deep oceans in her great, thick shell.

We feel utterly privileged to be watching her. It is a wondrous, emotional, truly spiritual moment. It's impossible not to consider the possibility – even the probability – of a Grand Design. And that somehow we all have a place in it.

The first line of Gerard Manley Hopkins' sonnet springs to mind:

The world is charged with the grandeur of God . . .

I kneel humbled before such grandeur. Tears prick my eyes and then cascade down my cheeks as Gail and I hug one another.

The turtle is so huge, so powerful, so harmless, so defence-less, so vulnerable. When she has finally finished laying we all feel drained, exhausted. This is catharsis in the true sense. We have come through glory and pain, and reached a deeper understanding of both ourselves and the role we play in the life around us.

This is one of the few times since her birth that the Leatherback will know land – feel the solid earth, the sand, beneath her massive body. The pull uphill from the sea is long on power, only twenty minutes in time. The whole process from start to finish – sea-to-sea – lasts over two hours. As she drags her great body back to the sea, orientating herself by the light of the surf, she exhales great sighs as she pauses to rest between each cumbrous heave. We will her along back to her natural element.

I have a moment of perfect recognition – that we are all part of the Universe. I understand once and for all time that there is an interconnectedness between all living things that cannot be denied.

Two years later, in mid-February, when the laying is over for the season, I am invited to go again to Rocktail Bay and watch another miracle of life. It's the hatchlings turn now – the Race for Life when the eggs hatch, and the tiny turtles, the size of a small bath plug, will make the perilous journey from the nest to the sea. If they are lucky, they will hatch at night, when the predatory seabirds are absent, and only the ghost crabs and beach-prowling jackals lie in wait for them.

Again we drive along a moonlit beach. But tonight the sand is smooth and unmarked. All is quiet but for the ghost crabs and the soft sound of the gentle surf.

The next night we try again and suddenly, in front of us, mini tracks lead down to the sea, perfectly replicating the giant tracks of the mother we saw two years ago. But the beach is now alive with tiny creatures – perfect bonsai Leatherback babies rush towards the sea under a star-studded sky. The waves glitter. One turtle hatches first, and its movement causes the others to hatch. Their collective vibration causes the sand to sift down through this pulsating mass and to become impacted beneath them so that they rise up from the nest as if in a giant lift. One or two get lost or tip over the main scrabbling, fighting mass and are left to perish in their sandy grave – once a womb, now a tomb. I rescue one little one from the nest. It looks as if it is dead, tiny flippers dangling limply. It lies inert in the palm of my hand but as I walk towards the sea, its little body suddenly surges forward, scrabbles frenetically, flippers waving excitedly, nearly plunging off my hand as it feels the presence of the sea. Its tiny flippers now feel strong and leathery, its life force formidable. I place it on the sand amidst other scurrying babies all hell-bent on making for the ocean. They will not be stopped in their run for the sea. Their flight is instinctive, powerful. The hatching is over in minutes. The sea swirls up around the tiny bobbing figures.

'Stand still!' yells our guide.

Tiny turtles twirl and spin in the sea round my ankles. They are so small, so powerless – only one in a thousand will survive to adulthood – yet their instinct and resolve is so strong. The vast oceans of the world – south and north – await them; the

Leatherback is the only turtle to swim in both hemispheres. Years later, that tiny Leatherback turtle, now an adult female, after circumnavigating the globe many times, will come back to within 100 metres of where she hatched to lay her own eggs and thus repeat the process that has been going on unchanged for millions and millions of years. She will instinctively come home.

The baby turtles swirl off in the surf, flippers working desperately as they swim for the deeper water, and then the beach is silent and deserted. It is as if Mother Earth has hiccupped for a moment – the birth of the turtles an exhalation of her breath. And then silence. The beach is deserted again except for the palely glimmering ghost crabs and a solitary wandering water mongoose.

I am so overcome by the power and beauty of the moment that I ask to be left alone on the beach. I will walk back to the lodge when I feel like it. The others drive off and I sit alone on the sandy high-water mark, thinking about life and death and the endless cycle of existence. Of how we are such a small part of it, but interconnected.

And then I can't believe my eyes.

It's as if the Universe is determined that I repeat the experience of joy and wonder, and the knowing of my place in it.

A huge Leatherback – this must truly be the last of the season – is dragging her way up the beach and making in my direction. She must have been coming ashore for the last few weeks, and tonight is perhaps her tenth time this season. Over that time she will have laid over a thousand eggs. This will be her last clutch before she heads back to the great, deep oceans. I am incredibly lucky and deeply privileged to see her.

I sit still. She settles only a couple of metres away from me, lifts her great head and gazes directly into my eyes. I know her. She knows me. Although she is so huge, so powerful, and so near, I feel no fear. Only recognition. We are part of the same scheme of things.

She starts the long, laborious process of digging her nest as I sit with her and share her travails. Finally the nest is ready. She turns and looks at me again. Then she retreats into her trance-like state. As she lays, her body pulsates and I involuntarily strain with her. We have both given birth before. I place my hand on her icy back and encourage her, 'Come on. Nearly done. Well done.'

When she has finished laying she is exhausted, but emerges from her trance to gaze once more deep into my eyes. Tears are running down her great leathery cheeks. Then her huge front flippers slap against the sand as she fills the nesting hole. As the hole begins to fill, she tamps down the sand with her back flippers. Finally, when the nest is full, her back flippers softly spread the sand from side to side. When she has finished, it is as if there was never anything but sand there. She raises her huge, ancient head and groans. She is getting very tired now. And then she rests, her giant breaths sighing in the breeze that has sprung up around us. Her instinct has brought her home.

I think to myself that I must be one of the few people in the world who has sat alone on a deserted beach with a creature whose line stretches back for millions of years. I feel utterly at peace and at home.

Because, like the turtle, I now instinctively know where my home is. It's taken me a long time, but I've got there eventually.

My home is with everyone I know and everyone I don't

know or have yet to know. It's with everything I know and everything I have yet to know or may never know. I am just an infinitesimal part of the whole.

In the narrowest sense, my home is with my family and friends. It's amongst those worthwhile people (and I use the term 'worthwhile' in its fullest sense) who form a single nation among themselves, regardless of the country or background they come from. The people I feel I belong to and with – the Hon. Gwen, my English teacher of all those years ago; Indio, the Yaqui Pasqual Native American shaman I met in Tucson, Arizona; Daniel, the gay French-Canadian film director I worked with in New York; Alfred, Rita's Aborigine 'guardian'; Patrick, the dying Catholic priest in the Mountains of Mourne; Johnnesburg's Dan Rakoagathe, the Blind Prophet; Gareth, the Lion Man; Phrasongserm Kesaradhammo, the Buddhist monk in Chiang Mai; Laura and her two Chinese daughters, Savannah and Willow; the White Queen of Okoyong; my dear friends Vicki, Marié and Sylvia; and my family: Rita, Malcolm, Alan, Simon, Sarah, Tara and Tiffany.

And of course, Doris . . .

They have all touched my life and educated my heart and soul.

And shown me the way home.

BY THE SAME AUTHOR

There's More To Life Than Surface   Kate Turkington

'We must always acknowledge the interconnectedness of all things.'

These words of the Dalai Lama have an undeniable resonance in the experiences of the people we encounter in There's More To Life Than Surface.

How did the Dalai Lama's words impact on a well-educated cynic and non-believer who unexpectedly found herself undergoing a mindshift on a magical journey to the ancient sacred places of Peru?

Kate Turkington was that cynic and non-believer and she shares the experiences that uncovered the spiritual journey that she had, unknowingly, been travelling all her life, experiences that have changed her life in the richest way possible.